BOOKS b

UNINFLAMED (2022) 21 Anti-Inflammatory PRIMAL HABITS to Heal, Sleep better, Intermittent fast, Detox, Lose weight, Feel great, & Crush your life goals with a Kickass Microbiome

MASTER of YOU (2020) A Five-Point System to Synchronize Your Body, Your Home and Your Time with Your Ambition

BODY THRIVE (2015) Uplevel Your Body and Your Life with the 10 Habits from Ayurveda and Yoga

HOW TO
SCALE
YOUR
WELLNESS
BUSINESS

CATE STILLMAN

HOW TO SCALE YOUR WELLNESS BUSINESS

CATE STILLMAN

WELLNESSPRO
ACADEMY

Start here.

The Ultimate Guide to 3X Your Profit

For owners of medical practices, healing practices, gyms & fitness studios, and retreat centers

Go here:

—> wellnesspro.academy/start

* This revenue model only works
for wellness pros
who live their wellness habits.

A leader is best when people barely know he exists, when his work is done, his aim fulfilled, they will all say: we did it ourselves.

Lao Tzu

If your actions inspire others to dream more, learn more, do more, and become more, you are a leader.

John Quincy Adams

Contents

CAREER

VALUE LADDER

HUSTLE

SUCCESS

APPENDIX on REVERSING CHRONIC INFLAMMATION

FOR THOSE DEVOTED TO THRIVE

CAREER

THRIVE

Roxi carried extra weight and had allergies, depression, and PMS. She was a psychotherapist by trade. She had tried pharmaceuticals, elimination diets, and therapy. She had witnessed so many clients come to her with a list of symptoms and a diagnosis of an autoimmune disease that she was afraid she'd eventually end up with a scarier diagnosis.

Roxi also tried herbal supplements, meditation, and yoga. She liked yoga and bounced around with yoga teachers until she found me, Cate, at CLUB THRIVE. We seemed to know precisely what Roxi was up against ... and how to feel better. (See Appendix on Reversing Chronic Inflammation).

We have an understanding of how bodies work and also know the benefits of intermittent fasting. Roxi joined CLUB THRIVE, which was a significant enough investment that she was committed to showing up and getting all she could from me and our club experience. The psychotherapist met people who were serious on their path to enlightened health. She would still see her old friends, but she started noticing she had a better time with people who were healthier and more proactive about their lives.

In CLUB THRIVE, Roxi evolved her daily habits, including developing a daily home breath and movement practice, meditation, and cooking smarter for herself. For the first time in her life, Roxi had momentum with better habits to feel good in her body and happy in her life. She became increasingly uncomfortable with how limited her talk therapy practice was with her patients.

Roxi loved how she felt each morning upon arising. She could tell her habits were making all the difference. I guide my members into positive stressor habits, longevity habits, where they feel better and better. Our club members gained momentum fast because the culture around positive stressor habits was strong. Her sleep was deeper and longer. She no longer had cravings for crap. She knew the investment with our club was making all the difference in her future. Despite being an introvert, she was super grateful for the members she had become friends with. How I structured the membership made everyone feel like they were in it to win it... together.

POSITIVE STRESSORS

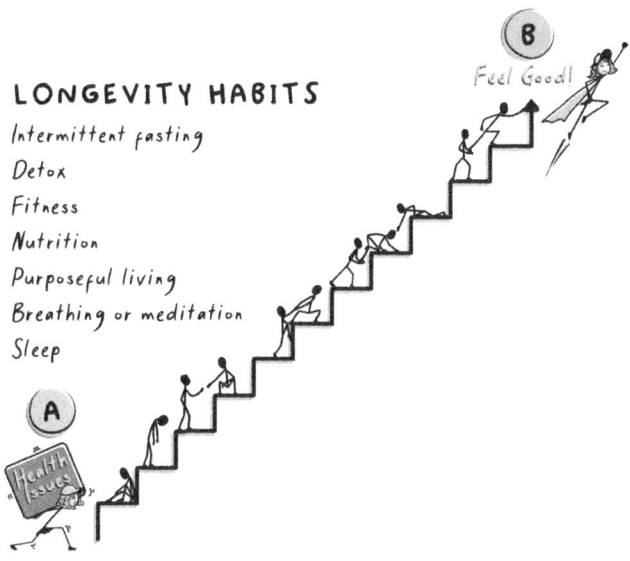

LONGEVITY HABITS

Intermittent fasting
Detox
Fitness
Nutrition
Purposeful living
Breathing or meditation
Sleep

In her new reality, Roxi stopped trying to control her body and developed her intuition. She noticed her old friends ate more, drank more, and watched more shows. While they complained more, they weren't interested in evolving. Everyone noticed they had less in common, less to connect on.

I addressed the differences between codependence and growth relationships. I also explained how people invest their time, energy, attention, and money. From a long-term health perspective, smarter relationships and empowered clubs centered on learning, habits, skills, and potentiality were simply smarter life investments. Roxi was saddened that she hadn't learned this at home, school, or psychotherapist training. It felt like time wasted, time in which she suffered many symptoms that now were clearing up daily.

Roxi could see how the prior investments she had made on her wellness journey... the time, the intention, the money she'd invested would pay off with each passing year.

Roxi reflected that wellness wisdom is truly the best life investment and commitment she has made. She wouldn't trade it for the world. How could she guide people through a life-changing experience, from depression, allergies, weight creep, and difficult periods to feeling amazing every morning? She wanted to guide those suffering from mental, emotional, and physical health issues.

Roxi wondered ... *why do some people, like myself, make the switch from sick care to well care? Why do some people save a chunk of their paycheck to invest in their body, mind, relationships, and personal potential?*

Roxi's work in 1-1 talk therapy felt increasingly limited compared to her wellness journey with her group. Her depression transformed into a steady happiness, not with Xanax, but with the habits that became her new normal from being a member of CLUB THRIVE. The lack of whole-body integrity in mental health care glared her in the face each workday. She realized her work couldn't just be for a paycheck and health insurance anymore. She needed to pivot. Pivot to impact. Impact to save her soul and redeem her real value to her community. Roxi decided she should make a difference. She wondered... *how do I genuinely change people's lives with my wellness wisdom?* She knew she couldn't counsel the patients on her habits.... or could she? She knew she had to change her thinking to change her opportunity.

HOW DO I CHANGE MY THINKING?

Then, Roxi asked me about Wellness Pro Academy - where we guide wellness pros to scale their impact and income with the CLUB model. I told Roxi about our members- the wellness pros at Wellness Pro Academy, and how we guide them through the CLUB business model as they enroll their CLUBS in real-time. Earn-while-you-learn.

This book is the beginning of our conversation.

The CLUB model works for psychotherapists, yoga teachers, fitness trainers, doctors, nurses, nutritionists, gym owners, and mountain guides. We've trained wellness pros to scale with the CLUB model... and align their impact potential with their wealth potential.

A to B

I'm curious if your story has elements of Roxi's.

What propelled you off the beaten path and onto your healing journey? Did you also shift from codependent to growth relationships? What is your wellness training? Is it holistic or allopathic, or a mix? I want to know who you are, dear reader.

Most importantly, what are your core lessons learned from your healing journey or wellness path?

Recall the training you sought, what you needed to know, learn, and experience. I want to know where you started and where you've arrived. That is your A to B, which we'll get into.

How serious is your desire to make a difference? Are you a careerist or a hobbyist? A dabbler or a lifer?

How do you define future success for your wellness pro? What's your desire? How strong is your follow-through? What are your current challenges? Take a moment and reflect.

I've been guiding wellness pros to success for over a decade. I've coached wellness pros to embed their purpose with a smarter business model. At the Wellness Pro Academy, we call it CLUB - the best business model for wellness pros who want to lead from their lived experience and their wellness lifestyle. CLUB gives you the infrastructure of a successful career that reinforces your leading by example.

This book will look at wellness pros from varying backgrounds and modalities, from allopathic and holistic doctors, pharmacists and nurses, mental health therapists, physical therapists, yoga teachers, personal trainers, and bodyworkers.

We showcase the club business model at CLUB THRIVE for people who want to thrive in their bodies and lives (even if they have a scary diagnosis or disease). We walk our talk and model the way for wellness pros looking to leverage their wisdom for income and in pursuit of transformational client results.

The main component of accelerating member results is building the right culture.

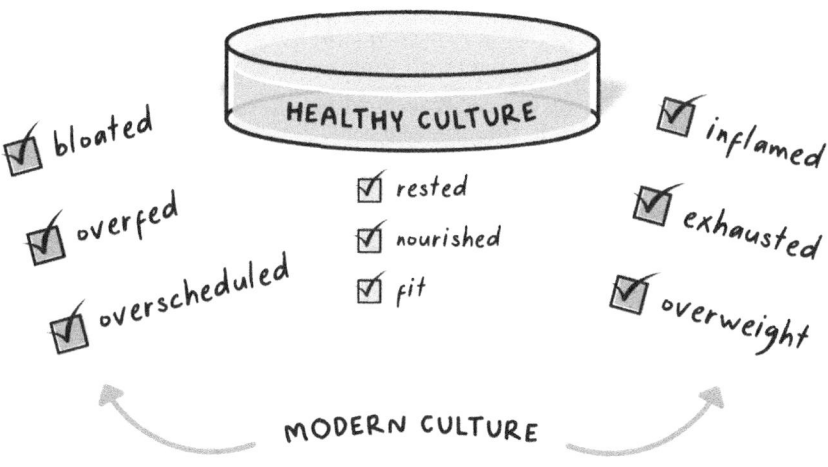

In your CLUB, you'll create a healthy culture to reverse modern culture's chronic symptoms effectively. As you read the next section, consider the culture you could create and the value that will bring to your future members.

YOUR A to B

Where is your value now? As a wellness pro, what transformation do you currently guide or want to guide?

This is your A to B.

Your A to B is the value you provide. This can be translated into packaging and pricing.

The value lies in the transformation. If that transformation lasts a lifetime, the value is exponential. The more value you can exchange, the more *impactful* your career will be. The better you can articulate the value of the impact, the more *lucrative* your career will be.

Pro is short for professional. Professionals exchange value for value. Professionals exchange the value of transformation for financial investment.

Most wellness pros leave impact and income on the table by *not* having a business model that insists on A to B. *A* is where prospects are when they become members.

A is usually struggling with the symptoms of underlying chronic, systemic inflammation. This may appear as stress, over-scheduling, depression, overwhelm, carrying weight, immune issues, trouble sleeping, trouble digesting–aka bloating; the list goes on. We'll explore this list in detail in the CHRONIC chapter.

A's habits may involve late nights, snacking, always being busy, eating too frequently, late nights from screen time, caffeine to wind up, and alcohol to wind down.

How do you guide them to feeling great?

B is feeling great. Physically strong. Well-rested. Deeply nourished. They are dynamically engaged with their goals, friends, body, and whole life. B has automated habits that reduce chronic systemic inflammation through all stages of life. At *B*, your clients sleep well, eat clean, and digest easily. They are resilient and adaptable and experience a baseline of positive emotions daily, every day.

That is a transformation. That is a solid A to B. A to B is a journey.

Your biggest value lever is to lead the transformational journey.

TRANSACTIONAL VS TRANSFORMATIONAL

Most wellness pros operate on a *transactional* business model.

Their clients pay by the transaction, which may be a session, a class, or a series. Neither the commitment nor the timeframe isn't enough to lead to results.

Wellness pros are *not* taught how to evaluate their client's health issues and goals and how to create a package based on goal-driven results.

The local and global marketplace can make or break your dreams. If you shift from a transactional to a transformational CLUB model - you uplevel yourself out of general competition. You simplify your marketing needs. You turn clients or patients into members. Members are empowered. Members part of a dynamic club are engaged, proactive, and supported.

To package a CLUB means to build a truly transformative experience. Members invested with skin in the game make it possible, but also scalable, for you to bust your impact ceilings... and income ceilings.

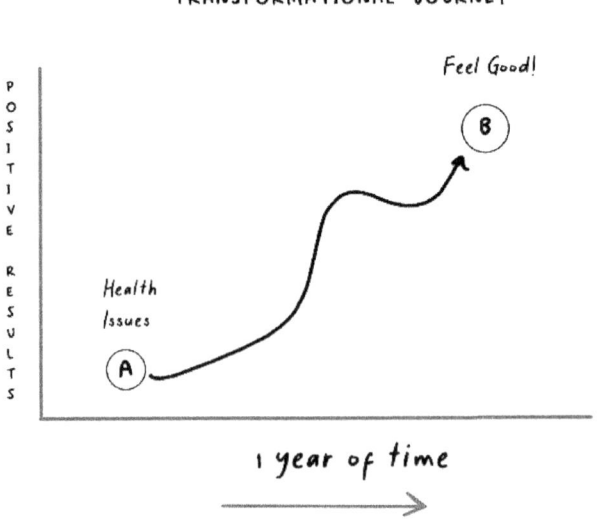

TRANSFORMATIONAL JOURNEY

And if you are a wellness pro worth your salt, chances you might be able to put together your journey membership right now. We find issues arise first with packaging and pricing. Next, with marketing. Next, with sales. And later ...with dynamic club engagement. And after that, knowing how to reverse chronic inflammation with habit evolution. This is why having a business coach who knows the A to B model is a wise investment with a good return on investment (ROI).

If you want a 1-1 wellness career coaching session, we can understand who you are. We'll help you clarify your values, mission, ambition, and business model for success. We'll guide you through a process to define your A to B. We'll show you how to design your potential Club, built from your unique convictions, mission, training, and ambition (It's free with PROMO code: PRO497).

GOLDMINES

Most wellness pros I've coached are exceptional in their care, body wisdom, personal biohacking, and subtle physiology understanding.

Yet, often, wellness pros don't know how they can offer the most transformational value to their clients. There are gaps. Gaps in their clients' commitment. Gaps in using technology. Gaps in developing an experience to guide people into their potential. Gaps in leveraging the collaborative potential of their clientele. Gaps in turning healing skills into a transformative journey. Gaps in their leadership.

You need to thrive–personally, professionally, and financially. If you aren't living your impact and income dream, you are less of an asset to your client community. If that is your goal, let's mine your gaps.

Gaps are gold mines of opportunity.

In this book, I'll show you how to mine for the gaps where you leave client results and a heap of gold on the table. When you close your gaps, you'll do the best work of your life, have the flexibility you want in your lifestyle, and reap the hard-won but truly liberating rewards of financial freedom. Plus, you'll receive my best, current insights.

I've led transformational clubs for over two decades. I've coached wellness pros into the scalable financial club model behind this career path.

I was successful as a wellness pro and wellness community developer early in my career due to discovering the CLUB model in my early days at the helm of Yogahealer.com. I'm devoted to wellness pros living from their lifestyle so people in our communities can thrive and have smarter choices to invest in a future of wellness versus sick care.

I'm known for telling you exactly how it is. As a futurist, an author, and a thought leader of east meets west, science meets ancient wisdom, I'm known for guiding my members at CLUB THRIVE to reverse chronic inflammation with primal habits. I'm known at WELLNESS PRO ACADEMY for guiding wellness pros into a career beyond their wildest dreams. Leading the club through a journey only they could lead. I love to be exceptionally useful to holistic wellness pros, as you love to be exceptionally useful to the people you most want to serve.

So, you need new skills.

You'll need skills in attracting, engaging, and enrolling your members. These skills aren't optional for those who want to live from a wellness lifestyle and avoid turning their wellness career into a daily grind.

Growth generally requires your growth. You have to reprioritize your attention and time for these new skills. These skills are leverage-able–meaning the better you get at them, the more time you'll have for your life. And you need time for your life. Your thriving lifestyle is what attracts people to you. You are the product, the guide, and even a member of your own club.

Four Problems

There are four problems with this transactional business model.

1. No defined results-based transformation
2. No invested commitment from the clients or patients into members
3. No scalability for leveraged growth
4. No service that activates the pro to leverage their lifestyle wisdom to create a healthy culture among their clients

Let's solve all four problems.

You have an opportunity to lead your way. Maybe you lead like a star, or maybe like a supporter, or even a mechanic or a connoisseur.

As an added income stream, your CLUB is an upsell.

INTRO to UPSELL

An upsell is when a client purchases something of a higher value and higher cost for an even better product or service. But let's start with the role of consults, products, classes, and challenges and then talk about your upsell.

Introductory offers serve the purpose of people seeing a better potential and finding out who you are. Introductory offers also do the most challenging work of assessing where they are and embarking on the initial personal upgrades. A strong process enables you to get to know, like, and trust each other and see if there is resonance. Your introductory offer, which is a process, should reflect your values, your integrity, and your personal body wisdom.

If you can lead a journey, a transformational CLUB annual membership, you can make a great living and experience a lucrative lifestyle. I grew Yogahealer by 50% during the pandemic because I had a club that met the needs of people wanting to become resilient and thrive through the pandemic. I had set up my CLUB, and people were ready for something better on the menu than isolation and a supply of toilet paper.

The upsell to CLUB membership can never go out of style if you can genuinely lead transformation. It'll never be too late to lead a CLUB with committed members to genuinely transformational results.

Why not?

Because the impulse to evolve is part of human nature. And those that can guide us to evolve are worth investing time with.

The member commitment permits you to work toward results straightaway. Momentum builds. Leading invites you to create the infrastructure for your members to thrive as a dynamic CLUB.

To figure out the club your clients want you to lead, answer these questions:

- When did your healing journey begin?
- What were your symptoms?

- Who were your guides?
- What habits did you develop?
- What skills did you develop?
- What made the most significant difference?
- What were your results?
- Who did you meet along the way?
- What are your core convictions or beliefs about healing? About investing in health? About daily habits or practices?

(Note: use the workbook in LEAD YOUR CLUB. (PROMO code: PRO497)

CLUB MODEL

As a leader, you are the living results of the transformation. You should be well rested. You should be deeply nourished. You should have the time of your life and live your purpose. Your self-care should become exquisite yet uniquely your style. You will model the way. You become the leader of the way.

This has nothing to do with chasing perfection or perfectionism.

This has everything to do with you being you and your integrity. The more integrity you have, the easier it is for people to engage with your resonance. This isn't about purity or abstinence. You leading the way is leading the best way you can, with what truly works for you in real-time. You'll be guiding your people to experience your level of thrive with more speed and ease by addressing the key factors that work.

As a leader already, you are doing this. With the right business model, you'll have the freedom to be your best you. (Plus, the business model scales from six figures to seven figures to eight figures.)

The two aspects–being the product and leading your CLUB–become the same. Both aspects continually hold you to a higher standard for yourself. And that is a life of integrity.

I speak from many years of experience. I tried purity and chastity and abstinence. I tried rebelling too. When you lead with authenticity, vulnerability, and living wisdom ... you will gain traction.

If you let yourself get caught up in the busyness, or wired and tired, or pudgy and inflamed, you make your success too hard. You can't sacrifice your quality of life. Or your practice, your health. Or your time with your kids or parents. Or travel. Or meditation. Or whatever lights you up.

To truly guide a transformational CLUB that earns a pretty penny–you need to be all in. You need to live up to your potential—no B.S. - no halfway. You're the guide. The leader. There is no way around it. To me, that is the beauty of the attention economy. You need to be worth paying attention to. When that happens, people invest. You live the results. That generates magnetism with people looking for that - whether they are aware of it. You represent.

Representing the results is a serious deal. You'll clear up a handful of personal integrity issues. Don't take it personally. Purification through leadership happens.

Many wellness pros are bumping their heads on a financial glass ceiling. Many are in a negative feedback loop of trading time–their most sacred possession–for not enough money to give them the lifestyle they truly want to live.

Over time, the loop spins into stress, from being out of integrity with the habits they know fuel their bodies and souls. At worst, they can end up with the same chronic stress issues as the clients they most want to guide. This is due to the wrong business model.

So what's the most straightforward key to success?

A key unlocks a door.

First, what doesn't unlock the door:

1. You don't need to sell online courses.
2. You don't need to become more popular, post on social media a few times a day, or run ads.
3. You don't need a pricey website.

The big key is the business model.

If you have the right business model, where you lead the journey to results, club members through your A to B. what is possible is a successful career on all fronts, as your lifestyle becomes lucrative.

Let me explain.

You are the product. Therefore, you must treat yourself as the product. As you do, you skyrocket your personal wellness and plumb for depth of integrity. You become more integrated... because, finally, the business model encourages you to lead from the lived experience. You are living in integrity with your wisdom. You stop chasing the little stuff at the expense of your peak performance and bigger earnings.

You'll have more time for rejuvenation and creativity. You'll be more committed because you'll only work with committed members. The real work creates less busyness, less stress, and more personal transformation for you and your members. More impact. You are earning more while working less, year over year.

I'll show you how. Before we get there–here is a quick review of a business model. Your business model is how you exchange services and products for money. You can't move your life forward if your business or career isn't set up to free up your time. You can't be as good as you could be at what you do.

You can devote your full ability to getting results for your invested members. Why do I call them members rather than clients or patients? Good question.

Members belong. Most patients, students, or clients come and go without commitment to evolve. Membership has an invested commitment. Commitment is necessary for transformation.

Transformation is worth the commitment and has a strong return on investment.

Thus, the business model is to lead a CLUB through a transformation. The most effective CLUBS work on annual memberships. Meaning members sign up for a year or not at all.

Transformation requires skin in the game. People want to evolve, to invest in themselves, their bodies, and their goals. People want smarter relationships within a transformational community. A CLUB lets you deliver on what people want - a place to evolve, grow, belong, and become their potential in real time.

Run your business to require skin in the game and give people want they need to feel how they want to feel in the future. It's that simple.

I'm not suggesting you build a BIG membership CLUB. Unless you like big. Most wellness pros I work with start with a smaller CLUB that is highly invested, connected, and a powerful container. As they get traction, their CLUB scales with them. We model the way with CLUB THRIVE, scaling with members-turned-mentors, and a small efficient support staff. This enables the leader, you, to lead by growing your wellness lifestyle. Whether you lead a big or small CLUB, there is leverage in terms of money and time.

Your club will demand your leadership. This means your unique skills rely on your unique ability, how you lead, and how you guide to results.

Your club will drive you to lead. Leading will mean you are listening. The dynamic coaching conversation is your personalized leadership development program. You are being paid in the process of leading. Not bad.

The good news is now you know the key. Now I can show you, step by step, how to set yourself up for the best work of your life. Your CLUB becomes your leadership development program, which builds greater integrity into your wellness lifestyle. You lead the way.

DHARMA

My name is Cate Stillman; I kicked off Yogahealer.com in 2001. This was eons ago, in internet years. I devoted my life to personal and planetary thrive, beginning in high school. By my mid-20s, I left a career in global environmental policy to spread enlightenment wisdom and primal habits to thrive.

I quickly became more financially successful than my wellness pro colleagues. As I earned more, I invested more in my wellness wisdom. More in my body. I prioritized my lifestyle business. I wanted to live my best life now... not save it for later. And I wanted durable investments that enhanced my future lifestyle. My version of that lifestyle dream includes living in two countries, two cultures, two climates, with two languages. My lifestyle involves biking, skiing, river running, and surfing with my core people. For the last decade, I've spent part of each year surfing at my subtropical home, skiing at my mountain home, and investing earnings from my clubs into fun homes and condos for my CLUB members to travel.

I've purchased highly desirable real estate with my earnings and maxed out my retirement tax benefits. I love being a mom, modeling the way, and creating opportunities with my girl and man. I can afford lovely homes, fuel my family's dreams, and do the work that matters most. For example, I'm taking her to Nepal for yoga and meditation training this summer.

Even more importantly, I live a life of higher purpose, of dharma. I have a more significant, deeper, more positive impact year over year with my members. I am more effective at what I do in growing people into leaders. I'm also well-rested, fit, and deeply nourished. I invest in my health and wellness wisdom. I'm at my fighting weight. I'm inspired. I'm focused. I'm productive. I effectively guide people through health, career, and life transformation. These are signs of having a business model and lifestyle model that works for me.

The wrong business model doesn't work for your lifestyle. It will eventually break you. The CLUB model requires you to lead from your wellness lifestyle, which paves the way for your personal and professional success.

Part of my dharma is to help wellness pros lead the way from their lifestyle. Modern culture is leading to chronic disease. The Wellness Pros are the sector of society most knowledgeable and experienced in cultivating healthy counter-culture. So, I'm putting my chips all in on wellness pros to lead us out of our shortening health span.

The CLUB model works for *your* lifestyle. Communities need their wellness pros to lead them to thrive. The degree to which *you* are thriving is the degree to which you can *lead*. Below is an example of a wellness pro learning CLUB from me and becoming a leader:

Erica McQuown
22h ·

Feeling so incredibly grateful for this program and format.

My goal for the year was to double my revenue of last year. And I just hit it! Halfway through the year - 6 months into the program.

What's fantastic is that I will onboard my last group in August, and then the rest of the year is setting the stage for next year, when my goal is to double again. And I totally see the possibility of this happening. This also allows for maternity leave with my third baby due in October.

Beyond the discomfort I've shared when reaching my edge, this largely feels like it's allowing for easeful living with the appropriate amount of growth 😌 Allowing to balance all the aspects of motherhood, while creating a sustainable practice and serving my larger community.

Don't worry, I'll be back sharing my lows again when they come. For now riding the high of gratitude! 🙏🐢

Carolyn Lang, Amy Heilman and 3 others   2 Comments Seen by 46

Leading by doing is most effective. I'll show you how to lead and earn for leading your CLUB. You can unlock your potential to thrive as a wellness professional. Your creative potential. Your wisdom. Your unique ability.

VALUE LADDER

INVESTED

Look back over the last 10, 20, and maybe 30 years, and do a quick tally of how much money and time you've invested thus far. Use the chart below to write down the line items. Your past investments are your foundation. Include the courses, trainings, workshops, books, online training, events, and plane tickets. Return to the beginning of your journey.

How Much Have You Invested? Exercise:

TRAINING	HOURS INVESTED	HOURS INVESTED	WISDOM/SKILLS/ COMPETENCIES

(Print the Workbook for this worksheet. Use PROMO code: PRO497)

Don't skip this step. You can't grow unless you know.

What you just recorded differentiates you from the people you are most called to work with.

Now that you are in touch with your investments and core convictions, you know the most effective messages to communicate. If you can't communicate effectively, you can't send a beacon to those looking for you. If you have body wisdom and can communicate, people looking for results can find you.

Combining your core convictions and wisdom investments, you'll see precisely how you can guide the best transformational journey and get paid a premium. And have the time of your life. Like I do. Like I've guided many wellness pros to do. It's all in the CLUB model. And the model relies on you knowing your core convictions and best wisdom investments.

Next, we'll look at the economic value ladder so you can see how you've invested in transformational experiences and how you can help others invest in your guidance through the transformational CLUB only you can offer.

5 STAGES

According to economic theory, let's find out why the transformational journey earns the most in the marketplace. Yes- that's right. It turns out that the economic value ladder - a concept from economics, can explain why guiding transformation is the highest value you can offer in the marketplace.

The Y-Axis differentiates products or services from undifferentiated to highly customized. (I'll show you how to be highly differentiated in today's wellness market.)

The X-Axis is priced from low to premium. (I'll also show you what to do to become worth a premium in today's wellness economy.)

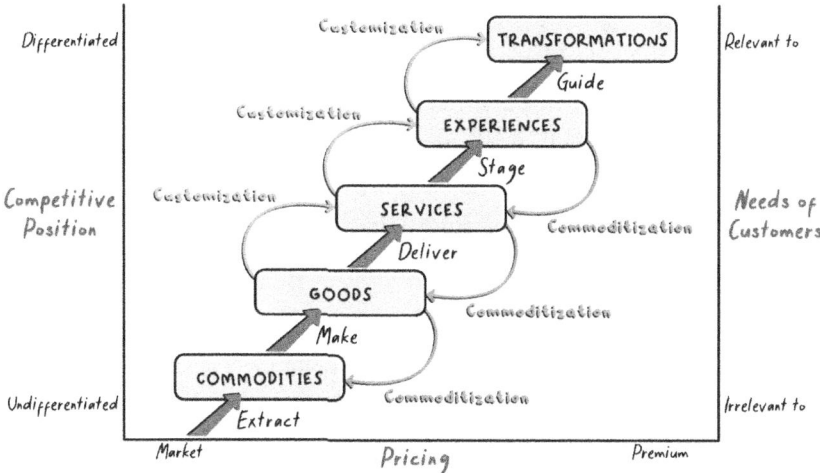

In the economic value ladder, also known as the Progression of Economic Value, you'll see that commodities to goods, services, and experiences that guided transformation hold the most value.

Humans value GUIDED transformation above all else.

See the progression of price from low to premium on the X-axis. See the progression of value from low to high on the Y-axis. Study this image briefly, and I'll guide you through each stage.

I hope that you'll understand that guiding member transformation through the structure of a life-changing CLUB is your path to a much better career.

The value ladder measures the historical stages of what we value most with our money as humans. It's progressive. There seems to be a natural evolution inherent in our economic progress. That gives me hope. Buckets of hope.

The value ladder is an essential economics lesson I learned from a business mentor. I would pay $1000 a session to coach me as CEO of Yogahealer, and I want to pass this on to you for a fraction of the price because I believe that wellness pros are best suited to guide transformation with a CLUB. If you pay attention, you may benefit as much as I have from taking the time actually to understand where your value intersects in the wellness marketplace.

Let's go through the stages one at a time. As we go, notice the shift from competition to increased freedom in pricing. This has everything to do with your future.

COMMODITIES

STAGE 1: Commodities

On the low side of what we value are extracted commodities—for example, carrots. Say you decide to make money selling carrots. You plant and grow them from the seeds you harvested last season. Once you've harvested your carrots, you've extracted your commodity. You bring your carrots to the marketplace to sell.

Now, a market price is established if a few other people are selling carrots at the market.

You probably won't sell carrots if you charge more than the market price. Commodities are sold at market price because they aren't very differentiated. Your heirloom purple carrots versus your farmer's neighbor's heirloom purple carrots aren't going to be different enough to demand an additional value at the market. Now, if more people are selling heirloom purple carrots than buyers want at the time, the price also goes down as you compete with your neighbor for the same limited buyers. Thus, commodities have a low value. Many gym classes and online courses fall into the commodity category right now. People compare prices. The market is saturated.

As humans got better at extracting commodities, some people got wise. They realized that for a commodity to be of higher value, it needed to be turned into something of higher value. Now, remember back in human history, once upon a time, we had fewer goods and services.

Lesson: Money buys basic stuff we need to make other stuff. The more basic–the more competition–the less profit margin.

GOODS

STAGE 2: Better Goods

People who bought the commodity would often make something with it. Think carrot soup. This making of the goods takes time. If you value time, if time is money for you, you are more willing to pay for the ready-made good. With commodities flooding the market, some smart people started to use their time to turn commodities into goods.

When someone came to the market with carrot soup and someone else paid more money than the price of the carrots, the economic progression ladder advanced a rung. Now, say your other neighbor also makes carrot soup. Yours is a carrot potato soup. Theirs is a carrot coconut curry. And you notice that people like her soup more and pay more for it. She has a higher profit margin. You are witnessing how differentiation affects pricing ... and profitability.

Additionally, someone who loves carrot soup but **doesn't have the time to make it, and has the money to buy it,** is experiencing more value thanks to the evolving marketplace. And that is the second stage. What does this have to do with you earning more?

If you can help someone on their wellness journey in a way that saves them time, you increase your value... and your ability to earn more.

If I can help someone lose 50 pounds in a year *and keep it off for the rest of their life,* it's better than if that takes five years to lose the 50. It's better for the person who has four more years to enjoy the benefits of optimal body mass and energy. They have a new lease on life. Their relationships get better and better.

How much money is it worth to a person over the next decade to feel good vs. have poor health?

Have you asked? That question is worth asking anyone you could help that is currently not feeling great.

Let's use another example—chronic pain. Think of someone that has had chronic pain and been on pain medication with side effects for a decade. Say I can help them reduce their pain by 50% and get off the drug, which they want to do due to the adverse side effects. Is it better if we can do that in a year, or if that takes us five years? Well, if you're in chronic pain, it's pretty clear that the sooner you are out of pain, the better. We've all experienced that.

Okay, so now we know that time matters.

Lesson: Money buys time. With money, a person will usually choose to get their needs met with greater specificity.

Let's go to the next stage.

SERVICES

STAGE 3: Services

So to review, from #1 to #2, we went from just growing and selling carrots to making something better. Coconut curry carrot soup. Think about it–someone not only planted, grew, and harvested the carrots, but they also cooked the soup. Anyone with money to spare knows what they are willing to pay to have ownership over their time. (And if you enjoy cooking over housecleaning, apply this to the service of housecleaning!) Anyone who knows that time is of the essence in their life will pay more for speed. Stage #3 saves someone even more time by delivering a service.

Not only does your client want carrot soup, but your client doesn't have to go to the market. She can get it delivered.

A friend of mine here, where I'm writing from in Alta, Wyoming, had a boutique homemade soup delivery company.

She made the homemade soup and delivered it to her soup club members weekly throughout the six months of winter. The soup costs more than carrot soup in the grocery store. She used her recipes. She sourced local organic ingredients. Her soup was of the highest quality (higher economic value) and was delivered (saves more time). Holy cow! What is happening here? Economic value is going from low to high, driving prices higher in exchange for time. And you couldn't get soup like hers, except from her, ... think differentiation.

Pay attention so you can apply this to your wellness career. Pay attention, and you'll see the highest rungs of economic value where you can provide the unique value–unique to your wisdom and character– with the most ease.

But, before we get to where your highest value and quickest path to earning more and being of greater value to your clients is, you need a solid grasp on stage #4.

EXPERIENCES

STAGE 4: Predictable Experiences

As economies evolved and people had more money *and* time, they wanted remarkable experiences. The more the experience met their specific desires, the more they would pay.

In the economic value ladder, this next stage is called Staged Experience.

For example, I was just at my place in Punta Mita, Mexico. An event was happening down the road at the Four Seasons called *Gourmet and Golf.* (I bet you're wondering if they served a spicy cilantro carrot gazpacho paired with a riesling!)

Gourmet and Golf is the epitome of a staged experience. It happens in multiple locations each year. Famous chefs are flown in from around the world to the Four Seasons' gorgeous golf courses. Rich people sign up for a guaranteed fabulous casual tournament experience.

At the end of each hole, you have a chef, a dish, and a wine pairing. You zoom around in your golf carts with your three other friends. You get a lovely buzz that takes the emphasis off the golf and onto the fabulous experience itself. The views are divine. The weather is perfect. Your friends are well dressed. The food is exquisite. The wine is well-paired. You are *having an experience.*

Later you talk to a friend who is also loaded and enjoys casual competitive golf with gourmet pairings. She also threw down her credit card for *Gourmet and Golf.* Her staged experience happened in Carmel, USA, not Punta Mita, Mexico. You compare notes. You compare chefs. You compare experiences and realize that you more or less enjoyed the same experience. You could each recommend the experience to a third friend and describe it accurately. *Gourmet and Golf* ultimately aims for... a reliable product and a predictable experience. So predictable... it seems staged.

How does this apply to you? Your ideal clients may or may not be the *Gourmet and Golf* clientele. That is irrelevant—hippies and Millennials alike through down fat cash for Coachella or Burning Man. Boomers take cruises. Yoga students fly to Bali or Costa Rica to go on a yoga retreat. Bikers rally at Sturgis.

If you are a seasoned wellness pro, you are probably hip to the limitations of staged experiences. Staged experiences feel staged. Take a Disney cruise, for example. Say your extended family wants to celebrate a 60th wedding anniversary. The easiest thing, everyone decides, is to go on the Disney cruise because of the gaggle of little kids in the family.

When you return from your cruise, your friend who recommended it to you asks you what went down. You compare notes. More or less, you had the same experience that everybody else has on a Disney cruise. Pictures of the grandparents and grandkids with Minnie and Mickey. Pants fit a little snugly due to that ever-replenishing buffet table.

Lesson: Staged experiences are well packaged and predictable, yet rarely personal enough to become transformative.

Now, think about this. Recall the wellness pro training you had. Were they staged experiences? Or was there something unique and special, so it wasn't staged?

What's the difference?

> The best, most valued personally transformative experiences are tailored to your unique end goals.

As you can see on the sheet here, the next place it goes, number five, is the highest. This is where the highest value is exchanged. And, fascinatingly, the most enjoyable and easiest earnings for the wellness professional is to guide invested members through a transformational experience. This will be the most gratifying, creative, and rewarding work of your life.

Drumroll, please ...

HUSTLE

CONVICTIONS

Health is the effect of a healthy lifestyle and healthy habits. Disease is the tree sprouted from unhealthy habits.

Dr. Vasant Lad, Ayurvedic guru

Your convictions are statements about your core beliefs. If you're not in touch with your core convictions, you don't know your most effective messages to communicate. If you can't communicate effectively, you can't send a beacon to those looking for you. And yes, if you have body wisdom to share, you'll find people looking for you.

Socrates made a stand for developing one's wisdom and stating one's beliefs, like his belief about why to put up walls. In conclusion, I'll review beliefs I've arrived at through twenty years of experience that resulted in CLUB THRIVE and the Wellness Pro Academy.

Your convictions are what you take a stand for. If you take the time to know your convictions, write them down, and articulate them, you can speak to your own journey and results *with conviction*. When you speak *with the conviction your results deserve*, you open the gate to next-level success.

Take a moment to consider.

What do you stand for?

What are your convictions about your health and wellness?

What are your convictions about investing money in body wisdom?

Conviction relies on experience.

What have your experiences confirmed about what is true in working with your wellness clients?

Write down your core convictions on health, money, and disease:

- _____
- _____
- _____

Your convictions will serve you in being more effective and more successful as a wellness professional. For example, here are a few of mine:

<u>Conviction #1:</u> Daily habits are the deal breaker between the global epidemic of chronic systemic inflammation vs. feeling good while aging.

As a wellness professional, you can make a stand for better habits for your clients to shift from modern health issues to feeling good. Wellness pros who lead their members into smarter habits get better results faster.

As a wellness professional, you are perfectly positioned to guide members to feel better faster when you lead a club based on anti-inflammatory habits, which are the backbone of good health.

Conviction #2: Wellness Pros who want to break their glass ceilings must invest in career training.

The essential career training is packaging the guided transformation, sales skills, attraction skills, and dynamic clubs ... in that order.

There's a reason most wellness pros reinforce their glass ceilings and get stuck. Usually, wellness pros aren't attracted to investing in career training. They invest in more yoga training–thinking they'll earn more if they are a better teacher. Or they invest in another modality–like a specific therapeutic training, like massage, Ayurveda, aromatherapy, or herbalism. If they invest in business training, it's usually general business training and not a specific coaching, sales, and marketing model for someone who knows the wellness-pro lifestyle business model, as explained here.

The internet is a very competitive place. Needing fewer students, clients, or members is essential for most wellness pros who want a wellness lifestyle ... not a business lifestyle. Career success is a different kind of wisdom, usually undervalued and under-invested.

Conviction #3: People transform faster in better company.

This is true for you as a wellness pro who can join the Wellness Pro Academy and your prospects who can get a ticket for your journey. As business guru Jim Rohn says, "Don't join an easy crowd. You won't grow. Go where the expectation and demands to perform are high."

Being with better company–the company of people guiding a transformational journey–who are mastering sales and attraction, who are astounded at their club's progress, would accelerate your progress.

Just like you wouldn't expect your clients to get healthier on their own, don't expect yourself to navigate next-level career success flying solo. Too many wellness pros try to figure it out on their own. Collaborative learning results in higher achievement, better retention, better ideas, faster learning, and higher level reasoning than traditional learning.

Look at your past as a wellness journey. Investigate your history as a wellness pro. You'll see that you probably didn't join an easy crowd— especially those who are very good at what you do. You probably invested in the best wellness training (and conversation) you could find. You found a way to make it work financially. I bet you joined your yoga training wholeheartedly. I would also bet that there was an expectation that you would grow, that you would perform, that you would show up, and that you would behave in specific ways. And I would bet that you stepped up to fulfill that expectation.

Now this same is true for your financial success. We need to join a crowd where exceptional financial success is expected. Perhaps join a group of people to grow their potential and income and design their lifestyle, year over year. In the CLUB at Wellness Pro Academy, this behavior is expected.

Because if we're not in that crowd, it's not normal to earn more. Learning more about a better business model or growing into it is not normal. Suppose you're in the crowd where it's normal not to grow, where it's normal to earn the same year over year, despite having more experience. In that case, your behaviors and personality will cement around that limited reality. You may start to think that you don't have what it takes. You may think the current market only values wellness pros so much. That breaks my heart. The sky is the limit. Aim high.

I value your body's wisdom at a premium. You prove your value by leading a club to results. So what are *your* convictions?

Guiding a club is less hierarchical and more infrastructural. You'll build the club, so the members connect. You'll be the leader... and a member. Why a member? Because you're living the habits, the vibe, the convictions ... and learning along the way. You'll have your growing edge, trials and tribulations, breakdowns, and breakthroughs. All of this makes a club dynamic.

Vibe. Convictions. Expertise. These are the golden words to guide a club to results. Your personality will shape the vibe of your club. Your leadership skills will evolve with leading your CLUB. At Wellness Pro Academy, we work on your dynamic club leadership skills with dynamic club structures.

YOU and YOUR GROUP'S POTENTIAL

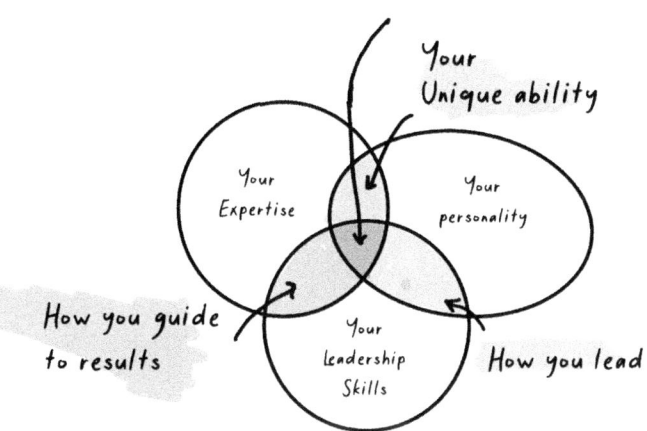

This requires less teaching and more around you as a leader who can rally a club around smarter habits with conviction, passion, and expertise.

And dynamic clubs are the fastest way to habit evolution. This means your clients have a better time and get the results they want, from weight loss to deep sleep to healed autoimmune issues. Members connect with accountability to your club's mission.

So, get clear on your convictions. After that, you'll see precisely how you can guide the best transformational club and get paid a premium. And have the time of your life. Like I do. Like I've guided many wellness pros to do. It's all in the business model. And the model relies on you knowing your core convictions.

UNIQUE CLUBS

Education is the kindling of a flame, not the filling of a vessel.

Socrates

Now that you understand how valuable your skills are in guiding transformation, you should put your hustle into designing a CLUB for the people you feel most called to lead. Most often, the first hustle is to build the CLUB - the CLUB only you could lead - into an offer. Before we get to packaging, let's review.

To guide someone through a transformation, they must be committed to the CLUB. You need to be committed to leading. The start point and end point must be clear. The length of time for the commitment must be concrete. The end goal must be agreed upon. The investment must be a firm reflection of both parties' commitment.

Your CLUB offer must explain the following:

1. The result of the transformation
2. The one-year membership requirement
3. How it works
4. The investment

Until you clarify these essentials, you'll work harder for fewer results or less money.

> You can't guide transformation until you package it into an offer.

Part of the reason I've been a financially thriving wellness pro for 20 years is that I've always paid close attention to what my people need most. I've designed the following questionnaire for you to become more relevant to your future CLUB members. Here are ten questions you need to answer.

Questions to Build Your Best Club

What do the people who you want to work with need the most?

1. What skills do they need to learn?
2. What beliefs do they need to change about themselves and their future?
3. What obstacles are in the way of their transformation?
4. How can you make the most effective and enjoyable wellness results of their life?
5. How can you save them time?
6. How can you save them money?
7. How can you measure their progress?
8. How long will it take for them to experience transformational results?

9. How long will it take for them to live the habits that lead to those results?

(Print the CLUB Workbook for this worksheet. Use PROMO code: PRO497)

To empathize with your future members, you might run the questions above through an empathy map. What are your future members feeling? Thinking? Seeing? Hearing? Doing?

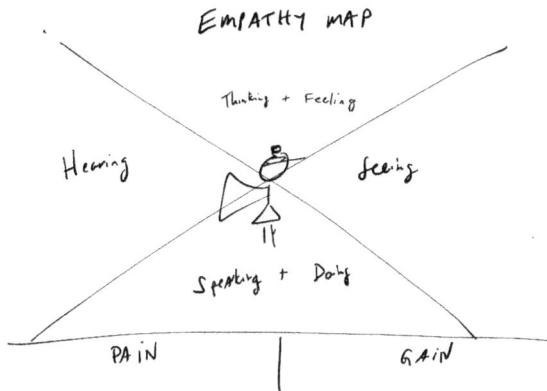

If you don't take the time to answer these questions, you'll continue to hit your head on a glass ceiling with time, income, or impact. You won't be able to guide transformation effectively. You won't earn more in less time from your wellness lifestyle. So, take the time now. Answer the questions. In the process, you'll discover your relevance to the people you want to serve.

You'll also notice how customized and unique of a CLUB you could lead. You are moving from offering services to offering experiences to providing a transformation. Each step of the way demands increased customization. Because you don't need to work with the masses, you can go hog wild in your customization based on how best you can serve your people. Keep in mind–you are evolving from delivering a service to guiding a transformational journey.

Pay close attention to what your people need the most.

Commodities (Extract) > Goods (Make) > Services (Deliver) > Experiences (Stage) > Transformations (Lead)

Reflect on this–you can only guide the journeys you have walked. Who are you a few steps ahead of? For example, due to my training and work experience, I guide 2 CLUBS:

- CLUB THRIVE: to thrive in your body and achieve your unique life goals
- CLUB at WELLNESS PRO ACADEMY: thrive in your wellness career by leading your unique CLUB from your wellness lifestyle

I've walked these two paths for so long that I know each bend of the trail. I know the specific obstacles that will arise for my clients along the way. I understand where new members are stuck and how to guide them through the challenges to results. The better you can guide your CLUB members, the more relevant you become.

Now, YOU only need to guide one CLUB.

To help you benefit from my lessons learned along the way, I'll give you an overview of how I built CLUB THRIVE from my convictions, the vibe I like, and my expertise.

CLUB THRIVE

Who is it for?

Adults who want to invest in their future self now- body, purpose, lifestyle, network, networth.

What problems do they have?

No process for making their future better in a significant way, quickly, efficiently, and with support for massive ROI, life-changing ROI

How does it work?

Six core crash course to get you building skills to heal, sleep better, intermittently fast, detox, lose weight, feel fantastic & crush your life goals with a kickass microbiome. Get one year of support for weekly coaching, monthly Q+A with Cate, and bi-monthly dynamic club sessions. Live sessions integrate four breakthroughs (detoxes/challenges) each quarter. The dynamic community of coaches, mentors, and peers at Club Thrive lead Circadian Rhythm/ Anti-inflammatory/ Primal habits and lifestyle design.

Imagine a CLUB that: (CONVICTIONS)

- Evolves your daily rhythm to free up your energy, time, and money
- Lines up your daily habits with your life vision
- Guarantees four breakthroughs/ year with challenges and detoxes integrated into the experience
- Guides you with life strategy; supports you through implementation

Imagine a CLUB that: (VIBE)

- It feels like dropping into the best conversation you could be in
- Surrounds yourself with people that have the habits you want next

- Focuses you on investing in your better future: integrity/body/lifestyle/career/purpose/relationships/wealth

Imagine a CLUB that: (EXPERTISE)

- Supports you to nail your individual and collective goals for life-changing ROI
- Normalizes smarter structures in your relationships to grow towards thrive, purpose, connection, impact
- It feels like dropping into the best conversation you could be in

CLUB THRIVE Investment: $6,700 /year

For how we permanently reverse the symptoms of chronic inflammation in CLUB THRIVE- see the Appendix on Reversing Chronic Inflammation.

POSITIVE STRESSORS

Next, we'll look at the convictions, vibe, and expertise of the CLUB at Wellness Pro Academy:

THE CLUB at WELLNESS PRO ACADEMY

Who is it for?

Wellness Pros who want more time, more profit, and faster client results

What problems do they have?

Time/Money constraints on lifestyle and profit margin. Too busy for their desired wellness lifestyle. Don't have an ambitious and strategic wellness pro collaboration network.

How does it work?

6-core crash course to get your CLUB set up, earning, and running. Launch your club within the first three months. Get one year of weekly coaching and collaboration support from WPA coaches and colleague network at WPA Club, who are all working the CLUB model—led by Cate Stillman.

1. [WISDOM] Your wellness lifestyle becomes your core leadership strategy. Activate your wisdom to earn. Because your wellness lifestyle becomes your core leadership strategy, you can deeply explore rejuvenation, resetting your rhythm with circadian habits. You'll experience spaciousness, abundance, focus, direction, and impact as you relax and lead your club. You'll lead from wisdom. You grow financially by maximizing your thrive, influence, and lifestyle freedom. You eliminate busywork and less profitable offerings; as you simplify, you enjoy your life and can scale at your pace.

2. [PILOT] You launch your unique CLUB in real time with our step-by-step guidance. And the camaraderie of your colleagues. You uplevel your wellness wisdom, your lifestyle, and dynamic club leadership skills. The CLUB model activates you as a unique leader. Earn while you learn. The CLUB is built to earn a return within three months.

3. [WAITLIST] You sell out seats and build a waitlist of future club members.. Lead from your personality, zone of genius, and how you fascinate to create a club that is magnetic to prospective members. Be guided with or without paid advertising, email newsletters, video sales letters, organic youtube, and local and social engagement. Use our templates to launch faster.

4. [MEMBER RESULTS] Your members will get results faster in your CLUB. You will be more effective because you leverage the power, structure, the intelligence of dynamic clubs. Coupled with circadian rhythm habits, reversing chronic inflammation, laser coaching, and habit evolution training... your CLUB will become notoriously successful. Leverage our training resources and templates with your members if you want.

5. [LIVE] [NETWORK] In WPA CLUB, you are hanging in *the* CLUB for wellness pros. We lead by example. Our club leads the club model. Our wellness pro CLUB members have so much in common. Yet, you're all unicorns... highly specialized in your wellness wisdom. Get connected to your peers in the connection economy...We're a network that is activated by collaborative intelligence. The vibe is evolving and intimate, and your colleagues inspire you to break your personal and professional glass ceilings. Experience the power of showing up as you, a wellness pro, in the wellness pro club.

6. [IMPACT] People thank you every day for showing up as you and guiding them through a life-changing experience. We're in the experience economy. Your job as a wellness pro is to guide the transformation. We live in an inflamed, bloated, diseased culture. You are part of the resistance, the future, the way forward. In CLUB, wellness pros have an impact.

THE CLUB at WELLNESS PRO ACADEMY Investment: $10,800 /year

The beauty of the transformational journey is that you can scale it if you want. Most wellness pros I work with at the Wellness Pro Academy are happy around the six-figure mark, maybe up to $150,000 a year. After that, they are comfortable and don't want to work more or add complexity. Many of the wellness pros we train stop less lucrative work in the desire to work with their more committed members.

Now, we tend to have over 100 members in CLUB THRIVE. The members like feeling the momentum and interconnectivity of our global community. They also enjoy the experience of being with people from around the world who strive for better every day. We use better leadership tactics so that all benefit from every live coaching session. Dynamic clubs are part of our WELLNESS PRO ACADEMY training to learn this skill.

Yet, most Wellness Pros prefer to work with smaller clubs of 10-30 people. . You get to choose what you want to lead and what you want to do with your club. Taking ownership of your personal preferences is part of designing your career, life, and the journey you lead.

Your club members will be empowered by the spirit, ethos, and embodied wellness wisdom your club provides. Some clubs are all online, while others are hybrid, with scheduled live events alternating with online coaching. Next, let's look at your CLUB OFFER.

YEAR

How long is a CLUB Membership?

My CLUBS run on annual memberships. I've tested ten weeks, I've tested three weeks, I've tested twelve weeks, I've tested six months, I've tested two years. I have found that one year makes all the difference. A complete cycle around the sun, a spin through the seasons, and a complete turn of the wheel of life is required.

Why?

I've found a few reasons for this:

1. People need time to transform.
2. Trust is built over time.
3. Each season brings up different challenges and breakthroughs.

People need a whole year to give the space and time for their most profound challenges. These challenges surface with time. If you don't have enough time, you'll witness the cycle of progression followed by regression. Guided transformation is life-changing when there is a vulnerability between the leader and the club. Vulnerability relies on trust. Trust takes time to develop.

POTENTIAL TO THRIVE

I've found it takes a year to lead for my members to have automated the habits that make them feel good. It takes a year. Therefore the commitment is one year. Time and commitment are the best buddies of lasting transformation. Engage in commitments that lead to results.

Now, at THE CLUB at WELLNESS PRO ACADEMY is also a year membership. Our members love being part of a committed, collaborative community, all using the CLUB model. Members appreciated the steady guidance to double or triple their income. Members underestimate the power of a community of belonging and becoming at the outset.

Also, I find most members start in a rush. Most come in overwhelmed. Having a time container of a year helps people relax and slow down. This paradox of slowing down and making small, steady improvements leads to more rapid and lasting results. To thrive faster and more efficiently, we must be relaxed and present with ourselves.

And most members don't want to leave after a year, so they renew. Just like members of a swim club, book club, gentleman's club, or health club - when you find where you belong, where you can become who you want to be next, and where you meet the best people, you're not looking to leave. The more you stick around, the more you grow, experience, and contribute in precisely the way that lights up your life. As an investment in yourself, the higher return comes from your commitment.

CLUB THRIVE is where I model the way based on my wellness lifestyle. I guide people into the circadian rhythm, intermittent fasting, microbiome diet, and other primal habits. At the time of this writing, a ticket runs over five grand. The habits are free. This saves members the money they invest- so it's a good investment even for those who need to recoup their money saved from the habits and opportunity cost. The habits don't cost money or are cost-prohibitive. If you have these habits for life, you save massive chunks of change. Besides saving money, members invest smarter in their futures and become aware of better opportunities.

You see, chronic conditions cost a person their potential. And you are always your own best investment. I aim to make my investments improve my life experience. A number in a mutual account doesn't do much for my lifestyle compared to a condo in Mexico. I can use the condo, rent it and accrue value at the same market rate as the mutuals account.

COST OF INFLAMMATION

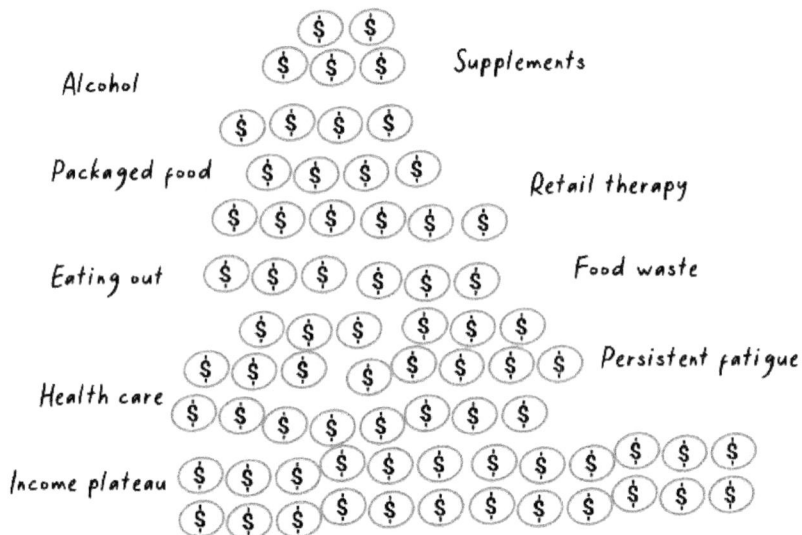

Our members report that their return on investment is exponential due to how the habits change their future. The habits are equal opportunity habits that generate opportunity.

But the five grand. $5000. That's a serious investment. If a future CLUB prospect knows the habits, why would you pay?

They could buy one of my habit books, like BODY THRIVE or UNINFLAMED, for $16 on Amazon.

If you could buy a book for the price of breakfast, why would you pay $5000 for a CLUB? If a person budgets $100 a week for food - that is their entire annual food budget.

For whom is this a wise investment?

For anyone that knows they are wasting their potential. For anyone whose health issues will cost more in the future.

SYMPTOMS INDICATIVE OF DISEASE PROCESS
#ACCELERATEDAGING

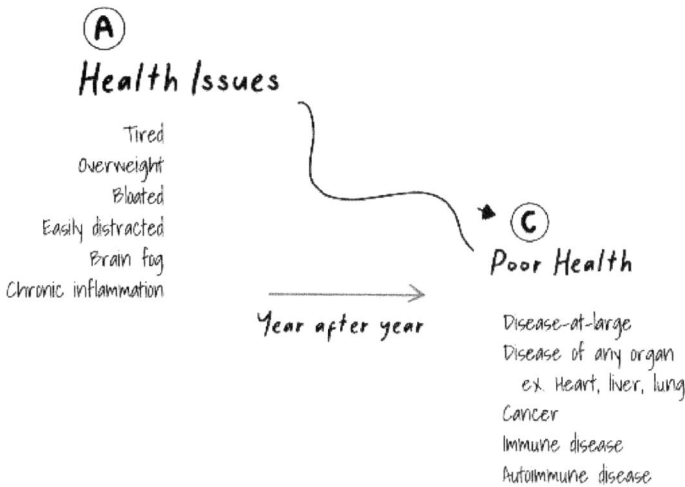

(A)
Health Issues

Tired
Overweight
Bloated
Easily distracted
Brain fog
Chronic inflammation

Year after year →

(C)
Poor Health

Disease-at-large
Disease of any organ
   ex. Heart, liver, lung
Cancer
Immune disease
Autoimmune disease

You'd pay because you take a chance on you. You want to make your investments improve your life experience. Because you want to feel good in real time. If you know your habits are leading towards more uncertainty and suffering and that you're not hanging out with people who can help, you have a decision to make.

And that is the same for our CLUB THRIVE members. The power of the journey, the community, the focus on results, and the success of past members... that is why prospects invest in the CLUB.

To lead your CLUB, your success will revolve more around your wisdom, enthusiasm, care, and ambition. What results would your members experience, and what will you need to do in your CLUB to get results?

The alignment of the who and the what are the first step.

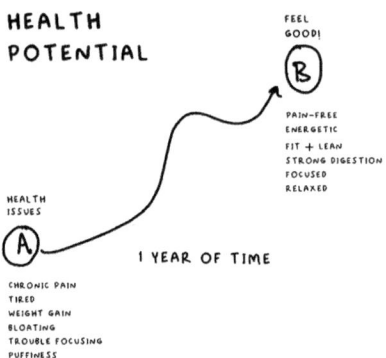

Typical results from A to B are in the image above. Typical CLUB members start bloated and overwhelmed and have trouble focusing their life and habits on what matters most and what leads to the experience they want. Some are in chronic pain - though sometimes the pain moves from one place to another. In the year, they shift from bloated to strong digestion, flabby to fit, chronic pain to pain-free, distracted to focused, and overwhelmed to relaxed. The $5k is a good investment for them because their future changes from pain to potential.

I tell you this because I couldn't guide my CLUB members out of their daily habits that generated chronic inflammation with how I was taught to practice holistic medicine. To guide them to thrive, I needed to guide a transformational CLUB.

Pause and ask yourself, what is truly at stake? Time doesn't stop. Habits compound–either towards the positive results of transformation or the harmful effects of accelerated aging and degenerative disease.

In the next section, we'll investigate the actual value of a truly transformational journey.

p.s. As a wellness pro, my background is in the habits of dina charya, the ancient anti-inflammatory, consciousness-raising, microbiome-enhancing daily habit rhythm of yogis. At WELLNESS PRO ACADEMY, some wellness pros use my curriculum. Others roll out their core competencies and core habits to their members.

YOUR CLUB OFFER

> We are in the results economy.
>
> Dan Sullivan, Strategic Coach

Let's build your CLUB OFFER. What journey would you guide in a year if you were strategically focused on member results?

A year. A year is a very long time. You have 365 days to guide members to results. You have 52 weeks. You have four seasons. What could you do if you were organized? What journey would you guide if you were strategically focused on member results?

Who is your CLUB for?

---------------------------- ----------------------------

What problems do your future members have?

-------------------------------- -----------------------------------

(If you want help - take the training with this book: Lead Your CLUB. Use PROMO code: PRO497 to get it free)

Like most online wellness pros, I use a combination of video training, live coaching sessions, worksheets, and a forum. I use SKOOL for our core competencies and CLUB hub. (Wellness Pro Academy, I supply training and materials for wellness pros who want to use my habit books and videos with their members to get a faster start to get their club going.

What experiences will you include in your CLUB?

You may have video training, online sessions, in-person sessions, live events or meetups, retreats, guest teachers, curated experiences, or VIP sessions. Let your imagination run wild. Some wellness pros I've trained incorporate garden parties, wild plant walks, art therapy workshops, and fridge overhauls. What would get your client results? What would enhance the journey?

How will it work? (What's included?)

Take some time to figure out your club offer.

------------------------------- -------------------------------
------------------------------- -------------------------------
------------------------------- -------------------------------

Imagine a CLUB that: (CONVICTIONS)

(What wellness wisdom, habits, and non-negotiables do you want your members to get from your club?)

_____

_____

Imagine a CLUB that: (EXPERTISE)

(What competencies do you want your members to get from your club?)

_____

_____

_____

_____

Imagine a CLUB that: (VIBE)

(How do you want your members to describe your club?)

_____

_____

_____

_____

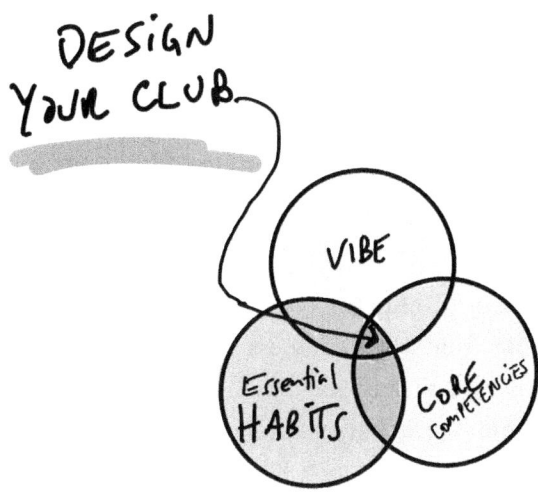

Convictions. Expertise. Vibe. These are the golden words to guide a club to results. This requires less teaching and more around you as a leader who can rally a club around smarter habits with conviction, passion, and expertise.

Transformational CLUBS are the stuff vision boards are made of. To clarify what transformation you could guide, create a vision board. Divide the board into two halves. One half is A. A is the pain points your ideal client currently endures. The other half is B. B is how they could be and feel if you had them committed to your process for a year.

If you are the leader of the journey ... what exactly is the journey you could lead? What results are you aiming for? What would you want the experience to be? Pause and consider. Daydream awhile. Be true to yourself, your personality, and your unique unicorn-ness. Jot down some notes. This book makes sense only if you take action by thinking, dreaming, and making it real.

How valuable could you be if you nailed the essentials of getting results? Again, which results are you aiming for? Focus on that.

Don't think about enrolling people into your CLUB yet. Focus on designing the experience to deliver the most transformation you can guide.

The transformation that you can uniquely guide is unlike any other CLUB. You are no longer "competing" because no one else is you. Because you are leading from your wellness lifestyle, you are at the edge of evolution. This also means you must own who you are and become of increasing orders of integrity with yourself–which we'll get to later.

> To lead a transformational CLUB, you must own who you are and become of increasing orders of integrity with yourself.

Build your CLUB OFFER for a lasting return on investment. Design a CLUB experience they couldn't get elsewhere. Become more and more relevant to the people that you're working with. As you do, you increase your customer relevance by becoming more relevant to your future members. They will want to continue with you and refer their friends and family.

CLUB EXAMPLES

It takes considerable courage to work in an environment in which one is compensated according to one's performance.

Dr. Thomas Stanley

Dr. Stanley is laying down a hard truth right there. You are compensated based on your performance. If you can guide to results, pricing-based performance can be a lot of fun.

Dr. Thomas Stanley goes on to talk about courage and risk: "Courage can be developed. But it cannot be nurtured in an environment that eliminates all risks, all difficulty, all dangers... Most affluent people have courage. What evidence supports this statement? Most affluent people in America are either business owners or employees who are paid on an incentive basis.

If you've read this far, you're investing your attention in your success. Let's look atLead Your CLUB strategies based on differentiated professional skills. In the Wellness Pro Academy, we've guided pros of all sorts, including nurses, doctors, healers, Ayurvedic practitioners, Chinese Medicine practitioners, bodyworkers, massage therapists, physical therapists, mental health therapists, energy therapists, midwives, and healers. Pros join WPA to master their CLUB OFFER, sales, leads, and coaching members to success in a dynamic club.

In this section, I'll share a few ways of pricing CLUBS. There is tremendous variability in pricing, which depends on your experience.

Pilates Teacher. TRAINER. Health Coach.

When Monica first launched her club, she wanted to transition from her day job at an institution and focus on guiding people to feel much better. She priced at $4000, signed up 15 people, and had the revenue to quit her other job. She couldn't believe how much more time she had with her business than with her day job–for the same amount of income. She also knew she had leverage to expand her club or the journey.

Her large living area would fit 15 people, and she wanted a familial atmosphere. She included club parties where she guided her members through interactive life-growth workshops using tools like liberating structures and collaborative learning. She worked out a deal with the gym where she taught so that her 15 members could get her classes unlimited. She wanted a close relationship with her 15 members throughout the year. She also wanted her members to have access to her 1-1 work as a personal trainer once a month for thirty minutes and 30 minutes of personalized health coaching.

Monica's Club: 15 people at $4000

- Body habits coaching: club weekly
- Four two-day intensive retreats
- 12 club night parties

- Unlimited fitness classes with Monica
- 1-1 habit coaching and personal training: monthly check-ins
- club forum
- Video Library - General and personalized

BIG STUDIO OR GYM OWNER (YOGA/PILATES/CROSSFIT/MOVEMENT)

Mari and Tom had a gym, three fitness rooms, three bodywork treatment rooms, and a juice bar. They could fit 50 mats in their largest room. Their gym had a staff of 10 trainers, teachers, and bodyworkers, who all operated as contractors. They were the only employees in the business, and both Mari and Tom had backgrounds in exercise physiology, personal training, and yoga.

They knew their members needed wellness coaching. They also realized they had no upsell to their fitness classes and were hustling to make a profit. They wanted a big club–50 members!

They already had one-day intensives at their gym that were unpredictable to fill. They decided to leverage their overhead and all the activities they were trying to fill. They wanted their members to have access to all classes and to be able to reserve a spot in workshops. They know their people are busy and can't attend everything anyway, so why not have many options? Mari wanted to use the juice bar for healthy eating classes.

Physical Therapist. BODY MECHANIC. Midwife. Detox therapist. Private Retreats.

Ann wanted to transition from her life's work in midwifery. She knew deep down there was a next level of her career. She was an expert in herbalism, yoga, and women's body wisdom. She decided to lead a women's empowerment club. In the Wellness Pro Academy - which guided her through transitioning her career–she earned more money and had more fun without the late nights of midwifery work. In the second year, she increased her price, based on results, and continues to break her records for rewarding career and income. She loved leading ritual events - and made that the cornerstone of getting her club together in person.

Ann's JOURNEY Club: 25 people at $6500

- Body habits coaching: club weekly
- Six, one-day women's wisdom + ritual workshops intensives
- Two, three-day body empowerment retreat
- club forum
- 1-1 health coaching sessions, 6/year
- Video Library - General and personalized

Jack was an all-star body mechanic. When we met, Jack had 30 years, yes, 30 as a massage therapist. He also was an Ayurvedic practitioner and detox specialist for ten years and had just completed training as an osteopath. Jack was plenty busy when we met, his schedule packed with clients. However, Jack was frustrated because there was no leverage in his business. He was trading time for money. Also, his private retreat detox clients would have a tremendous experience but could not maintain their results independently.

Jack packaged the journey to guide to results. He knew his patients needed life skills, breathing skills, cooking skills, and movement skills. He brought these skills in with a video library and two three-day live events at a local gym with a kitchen. He realized he only wanted to work at this depth with 15 people per year.

JACK'S JOURNEY: 15 people at $15k

- 6-day private intensive Ayurvedic detox (Pancha Karma)
- Body habits coaching: club Weekly

- Club forum
- Two, three-day super skill-building workshop
- 1-1 health coaching sessions
- Video Library - General and personalized

Mark's Peak Performance Package

A story...

Mark was a world-class physical therapist. He was tired of working with rich people and wanted to return to working with athletes. As we talked, it became apparent that Mark wanted to work with peak performers. Peak performers show up in all areas of life - from corporate board rooms to professional sports to amateur competitors.

Mark built his package for those with plenty of incentive to invest in their body and wanted a world-class body mechanic. He realized he was missing the health coaching component. He also realized he hadn't packaged his services to get commitment, investment, or incentivize his patients to get long-term results.

When Mark realized he wanted to work with peak performers, he knew these people valued their time above all else. A journey must be tailored to the needs of the members. His members wanted reminders, motivation, and personalized health concierge services to coordinate finding trainers on the road and working with other service providers.

PEAK PERFORMERS PASS: 10 people at $25k

- 25 bodywork sessions (1-1)
- Bi-weekly text check-ins
- 25 body habits coaching sessions (1-1)
- Weekly office hours
- Video Library - General and personalized
- Club forum
- Concierge services with other health care professionals

MENTAL HEALTH THERAPIST. Psychologist.

J.C. had survived severe childhood trauma. Her grandfather helped her get to college, and she excelled in writing. On her healing path, she found dance, fitness, and yoga. On her pro journey, she became a mental health therapist. In the Wellness Pro Academy, she put together an annual pass–she led the journey. And she started her book to help others with PTSD.

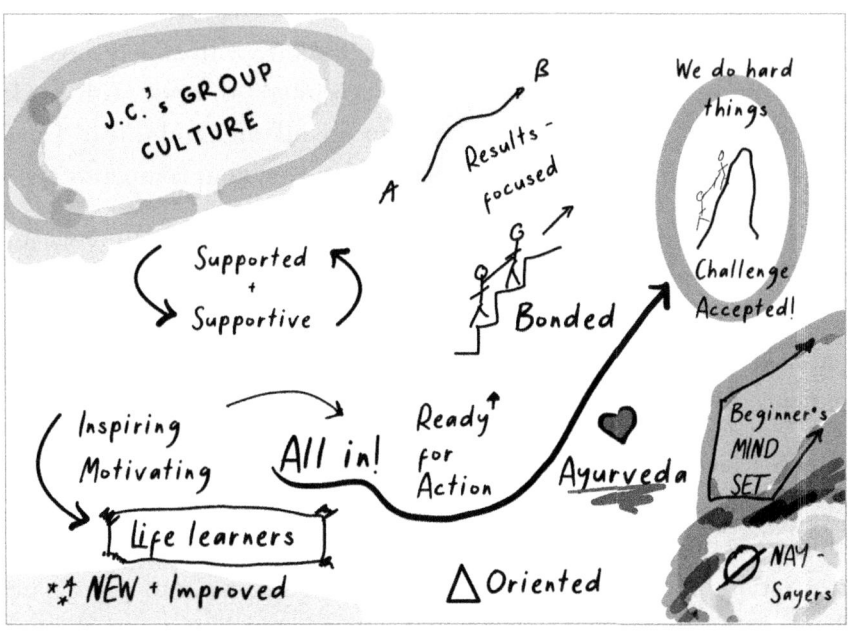

She learned how to run dynamic club interaction sessions from the Wellness Pro Academy. She found that her therapy clients loved the interaction. She noticed that the members could focus forward, make small changes that had significant results, and that her therapy skills and love of movement and physical health were finally combined into one offering.

J.C.'s Club: 20 people at 5,000

- Body habits coaching: club Weekly
- Monthly movement + magic workshops intensives
- Club forum
- 1-1 health coaching sessions
- Video library with movement and dance videos

NURSE

Annette was a lifelong nurse at a hospital. She had raised her three kids. She loved yoga and had a yoga-teaching side hustle. Her students adored her. She looked great. She was tired of nursing. Tired of the hospital. Tired of doling out prescriptions. Her habits were so different. When we met, it was clear that Annette was frustrated she couldn't make an impact with her wellness wisdom at work. More and more, she saw that degenerative habits brought patients into hospitals, and she wanted to keep people out of the hospital!

Annette kept her day job when she first joined the Wellness Pro Academy. She got her club off the ground, online, even while moving across the country for her husband's work and their dream of living in California. She loved the CLUB model. She got her CLUB off the ground, quit her day job, and never looked back. She fell in love with Ayurveda, aromatherapy, and skin care and added personalized products to her CLUB experience.

- Body habits coaching: club weekly
- 3-day intensive training sessions (Online or in person)
- 1-1 coaching: monthly check-ins
- Video library - general and personalized
- Personalized skincare
- Personalized aromatherapy

Nutritionist. Ayurvedic Practitioner. Chinese Medicine Practitioner.

Lorena had troubling acne as a teen and young adult. This started her on a healing journey in Ayurveda. When we met, she had already completed her training. She was determined to help young women invest in their body wisdom and lead them to the life skills she wished she had without needing to become practitioners.

Leanne's Club: 20 people at $6500

- Body habits coaching: club Weekly
- Three-day intensive training sessions (Online or in person)
- Skincare workshops
- Yoga workshops
- Personalized herbal formulas
- Personalized therapeutic sessions
- 1-1 Health Coaching: monthly check-ins
- Two club Guided Detoxes a Year
- Video Library - General and personalized
- Personalized herbal formulas

BOUTIQUE GYM OWNER (PILATES/CROSSFIT MOVEMENT)

Many yoga studios learned early on that Yoga Teacher Training (YTT) was a breadwinner that kept the studio in business. In the early days, studios could also depend on retail as a breadwinner, but as that went online, that income stream dried.

Leanne had a small yoga studio that fit twenty mats in a medium size town in Texas and had a retail space. Her YTT training kept her studio afloat. She didn't realize that was her upsell or high ticket item.

She had just turned 60 when she started in the Wellness Pro Academy. Leanne's following as a teacher was primarily women aged 50-75 who loved her infectious inspiration and body knowledge in the classroom.

Leanne knew she could fit 20 people, and that was it. Plus, she didn't want to work a lot. Her club filled fast. Having the container of the journey, having the one upsell, the one offer meant she didn't have to put on so many workshops or other events to help her most committed members. Because she loved doing local retreat-like intensives at her studio, she included four weekends of retreats for her members. She wanted her members to recruit new members, so she included eight, bring a friend member mixer free talks based on topics that her members wanted to learn more about.

GYM JOURNEY Club: 50 people at $5000

- Body habits coaching: club weekly
- Unlimited fitness classes
- Six one-day intensive retreats
- Bring a friend mixer free workshops
- Cooking classes
- Club forum
- Video library - general and personalized

Mari and Tom knew they could leverage their relationships with teachers, trainers, and therapists with a VIP pass that included one-on-one work.

GYM VIP Club: 10 people at $10,000

- Personal training package
- Bodywork/Yoga therapy package
- VIP health coaching 1-1 sessions

(We can walk you through designing your CLUB for free in Lead Your CLUB. Use PROMO code: PRO497)

PRICING

Once invested, the person's identity and complete orientation toward their objective changes. Because they now must go forward, they're no longer confused about what they need to do. They've already acted, and now they need to make good on that action.

Benjamin Hardy: *Willpower Doesn't Work*

For members to gain traction, they need to be invested. If your members aren't invested, you'll all struggle with commitment. You might be wondering what your annual membership price should be. Converting interested prospects into members is a sales skill, not an unconquerable barrier.

Now, before you lead your CLUB, you won't know what results you will get. However, you can look back at the work you've done thus far.

What are the trends in your personality over time? What do your clients say about their results since working with you?

If you haven't asked, now is the time. You want to know the results of your work. You want to understand the value, the savings to that person, the new opportunities in their life, and how their life has changed from your work together. You want to learn your client's stories and, soon, your members' stories. You want to be able to vocalize and repeat these stories to those who haven't worked with you ... yet.

When you can own what you know and prove the value of the transformational CLUB you can guide, you stop competing on price. Arguably, the value you will provide is priceless. When you ask someone who was in pain for years and now wakes up feeling like a million bucks what it is worth, they don't say a million bucks. They say the value of their healing transformation is priceless, that it goes beyond words. You should start to break those cost down into specifics.

You might wonder where we find people who want to invest this kind of money in themselves. Surprisingly, it's not the wealthy. It's people like you and me. People who want to invest in themselves, in their body wisdom, in their better, brighter future. Most people get that they are their best investment ... especially when things start to break down.

Your future members need you to set a price point that is high enough for them to have skin in the game. High enough for them to pay attention to commit to their goals and your guidance.

Your client needs you to set your price high enough for her to take the actions that will overcome her current habits and lead her straight to her desired results.

To price your CLUB based on the transformational results you can guide, answer these questions. If you haven't already, you need to talk to your clients to get their feedback.

- What results have your best clients had since working with you?
- What were those results?
- What are the additional benefits my client experienced from those results?
- How much money were those results worth to that client?
- Could I guide them to results faster now that I had a CLUB they were committed to?

Once you answer those questions, you'll have a ballpark number for the value of your CLUB membership. Value should exceed price.

Write down the ballpark price for your CLUB:

_____

One guideline on pricing I respect is from Dan Sullivan from Strategic Coach. Dan recommends going with the price that scares you and adding 20%. The reason for adding the 20%?

The added 20 percent is your commitment to yourself, your commitment to your value, and the proof that you're willing to go through a period of courage that might include rejection because you want to develop a new capability and be better paid for how good you think you'll be in the future.

Dan Sullivan, Strategic Coach

I have found in over fifteen years of coaching wellness pros that the reason for rejection is a lack of sales skills. A lack of prospects or leads compounds this lack of sales skills. Therefore, at Wellness Pro Academy, we focus on YOUR CLUB OFFER, sales skills, and leads to make this model work. With a solid offer, a steady lead flow, and exceptional sales skills, enrolling a few people per month is handsomely rewarded.

You want to price your membership to deliver a return on investment that is exponentially higher than the investment. And you, too, should want to develop more capability and capacity for how good you could get.

While your price depends on your experience level in guiding people to results, there are other factors. I've found with many wellness pros I've coached, the leadership personality they've chosen to develop matters as much as their level of experience.

Someone with natural self-confidence and a solid ability to connect with people can quickly charge more than someone shy and withdrawn, regardless of skill. Now, personality is shaped by habit. A wellness pro can dramatically improve their earning potential with habits that focus on confidence and connection.

A wellness pro can dramatically improve their earning potential by focusing on their CLUB OFFER, sales skills, and lead flow. Without starting a CLUB, with invested members, you won't build confidence built by experience.

Now, confidence in your communication is built like any other skill. Communication capabilities are most critical when industry turbulence is high. And right now, industry turbulence is high.

To improve your communication, follow this advice:

- Consistently and authentically communicate your care.
- Challenging yourself to achieve at higher levels.
- Grow beyond your previous potential.
- Effectively communicate your achievement.
- Witness your confidence soar.

SIGNS YOU ARE PRICED TOO LOW

Challenge yourself to charge what the transformation is worth. When you challenge yourself, you will get rejections. If you hold to your vision, you will also get clients with significant skin in the game. The price point must be high enough for this to be a serious decision, with total commitment. The cost of degenerative habits is poor health. Poor health is always more expensive in the long run.

NEGATIVE STRESSORS

Health Issues (A)

Degenerative Habits
- snacking or eating late
- sedentary lifestyle
- convenience food
- short term decisions
- worry, negative thinking
- sacrificing sleep

Poor Health (C)

Have you ever heard someone complain about the rising price of groceries and then drop $150 at a fancy restaurant? Or drive away from class in a luxury car? People are often irrational with money and spend on what they value.

Skin in the game

As a competitive soccer and basketball player, I was taught to have skin in the game. More often than not, I left skin on the field or the court. In psychology and economics, skin in the game is referred to as "escalation of commitment." Skin in the game is a sunk cost on the way to return on investment.

The hard choice for people to part with their money happens during the enrollment process. Once invested, people don't want to lose their investment. This creates an effect where if you can get people ready to invest in themselves, they'll be relieved once they do.

Without skin in the game, you can't get members to results. You won't get committed members if your price isn't high enough.

Wellness pros set their prices too low because they haven't invested in getting good at sales. Enrolling your members is sales. We coach Wellness Pros in sales at Wellness Pro Academy. We also coach our pros in getting enough leads to fill their CLUB.

Right now, consider how much skin you want in the game from your members.

How significant are the results you are willing to guide to?

Your price must reflect your desire to show up with your best 100% of the time. With sales skills, which are learnable, you will also get clients investing at a higher level.

The more your members are invested, the more value can be exchanged in your CLUB. On average, the wellness pros I coach want to guide about 30 people per year through a transformational CLUB. They charge a range of $2000 - $12000. The price difference reflects (a) their experience and (b) their confidence.

The more your members are invested, the more valuable your CLUB will become to your members.

If we return to the Economic Value Ladder from earlier, there is a third dimension to how people spend money. This third dimension is a plane called Velocity of Relationship. Velocity of relationship reflects the speed of commitment and trust. I've seen new members gain traction towards feeling good very quickly, members who I met for the first time in the enrollment process just weeks before. The speed at which we gained trust in working together had everything to do with knowing what results they were here to get with them and me having skin in the game.

If you understand this, you can work with people looking for results now and quickly. You'll be able to work with people at premium pricing. You'll be called into the best work of your life.

MOMENTUM

Sometimes you put walls up not to keep people out, but to see who cares enough to break them down.

Socrates

Next, we'll dive into how we build momentum in the CLUB model. Let me walk through what happens with CLUB THRIVE so you can get an idea for your CLUB. The journey I guide in CLUB THRIVE is to upgrade negative stressor habits into positive ones. We use the primal habits I outline in UNINFLAMED. For how we reverse the symptoms of chronic inflammation in CLUB THRIVE- see the Appendix on Reversing Chronic Inflammation.

New members are surrounded by existing members who have automated the primal habits. Primal habits are longevity habits that reverse modern humans' chronic degenerative issues due to diet and lifestyle.

We guide our members to automate intermittent fasting, fitness, and breathing exercises. Soon members have more energy to focus on their bigger life goals, which are also part of our core competencies.

Our existing members create forward momentum for new members. What I want you to notice from the image below are the people on the staircase. The staircase starts at **Health Issues** and ascends to **Feeling Good**.

POSITIVE STRESSORS

This is a natural outgrowth of better daily habits that emphasize being a well-rested, well-nourished, relaxed, and focused human being. Another positive stressor we use is detoxing. I've found seasonal detox foundational to releasing chronic inflammation from the body and a faster path to shift outdated mental and personality habits.

Momentum for our members is club generated. This means our club momentum is not reliant on me exclusively as the leader or any other member. Every member has access to this momentum all the time. Even me. And some days, I use the club's momentum to engage in the positive stressors that result in feeling good!

(Note: Before I wrote books, I used other people's books with my club members. Many of the members at Wellness Pro Academy use my books - <u>BODY THRIVE, MASTER of YOU, or</u> UNINFLAMED because they are organized in a way that is easy to coach habits. The subtitle for UNINFLAMED describes the research within 21 Anti-Inflammatory Primal Habits to Heal, Sleep better, Intermittent fast, Detox, Lose weight, Feel great, & Crush your life goals with a Kickass Microbiome.)

How many members to start?

Your club can start with just five members. It is essential to get your club going so it can grow. Failure to launch is real with wellness pros. Inside Wellness Pro Academy, it's faster to start earning by establishing your club because everyone else there is launching their club, too. You can work peer pressure to your advantage!

At the Wellness Pro Academy, we've tested quarterly and monthly enrollment for a decade. For a wellness pro in their first year with the club model, aiming for a 20-member club, quarterly enrollment might look like this:

ANNUAL INCOME: 100K

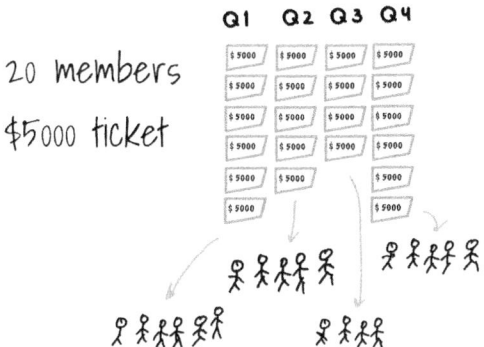

In the Wellness Pro Academy, we guide our pros to build a membership community where experienced members support new members. This is the fastest way for new and experienced members to evolve in leadership. We build this into the systems for growth for those who want to scale. Building with the end in mind is the smoother, faster path to success.

Discipline to the target builds the momentum of your club. You guarantee success by aligning your attention, effort, and actions with the club model.

DISCIPLINE TO YOUR TARGET

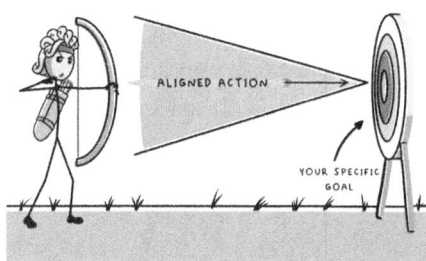

As members get results, they can measure their progress from where they started. With new members joining quarterly, it's easy to remember where they were when they started. The club grows as members get results and their friends ask about what they are doing differently.

BIZ PLAN

Where are your future members now?

Once you decide to make the CLUB model work for you, you may wonder a few things. Where will your club members come from? What will be their objections to enrolling? How will I get their attention?

First, let's clarify how many members you want to enroll per year and then break it down monthly.

1. How much money would you make in the next year if you were guiding members to results? _____

2. How many people do you want to guide per year? _____

3. Divide how much you should make by the number of people _____. This is the cost of your transformational journey. Your other income streams can help you connect with clients to become future members.

4. Divide the # of people by 12._____

This is the number of people you need to enroll per month.

For example: $/year = $200,000

1. People/Year = 40
2. CLUB membership = $5000
3. # Enroll per Month = 3.2

So, your enrollment number is 3.2 people per month. Month after month. As I said earlier, you can have a lovely lifestyle working with 40 people a year. If your cost of living is just $80k a year, and it costs you $20k in overhead to run your business, you could invest $100k per year. Not bad long-term planning!

The model scales. If you want 50 members at $10k, you have a $500k business.

In this example, you'll need to attract ten good leads per month to enroll the best 3 to 4 qualified people for your year-long transformation journey.

In the pricing section, I talked about increasing your prices as you improve your skills. As your transformational club gains traction, you may increase your price.

If that sounds outrageous, do you know that other wellness pros are earning this for guiding people to results? They enjoy their work because their people are financially committed. Everyone they work with has skin in the game!

You won't need to work with more people to make significantly more money. So, as you can see, these numbers are flexible. The important thing for you now is to focus on the right numbers as you build your skills.

I know of people who work with ten people for $25k. It's an elegant $250k income. If you are a highly skilled body mechanic and can lead to results worth more than $25k a year to someone, and you want a lifestyle career, why not?

> Price yourself at enough of a stretch that you'll show up with all you've got and continually improve.

Why make your life more complicated?

Now, if you are starting as a wellness pro and don't have much experience or confidence, I have a few pieces of sage wisdom.

1. Work with people you know you can help.
2. Price yourself at enough of a stretch that you'll show up with all you've got and continually improve.
3. Raise your rates as your value increases.
4. If you are already ace at what you do, acknowledge that time-earned accomplishment in every cell of your being. Build your sales skills, and read on.

THE SALES
CONVERSATION

No one's going to come to your house and make your dreams
come true.

Grant Cardone, Sales Guru billionaire

As you dial in your CLUB OFFER, you'll want to talk to prospects.
Starting with past clients is where you can get input to finalize your
offer and ask for referrals from clients to their friends who your club
could help.

Once you have your prospect's attention, you want to understand their
challenges. To do that, you need to set up a 1-1 conversation to know
their specific challenges and goals.

This kind of conversation is the beginning of your sales training. It's not
in the scope of this book to go thoroughly into sales training. In the
Wellness Pro Academy, it takes a few months of intensive training for

most wellness pros to get good at this skill and about a year to become masterful.

Remember, sales are a necessary skill if you are self-employed. Sales fall under the category of sales-generating activities. Sales-generating activities are what you'll do to sell out your seats. If you are committed to leading a transformative journey–know that the transformation starts getting traction in the sales conversation.

Sales conversations will make you a better club leader. Sales are the process of guiding people to invest in a better future for themselves.

Once you realize what is truly at stake for the person with health challenges leading to poor health, you may care enough to clear the hurdles that keep the person from investing in what will make them feel good in real time. Remember–you are helping them see they have two choices. "B" is the "feel good in your future" choice. "C" is the choice of continuing the trajectory they are currently on. Choosing "C" compounds health issues from their current habits over time.

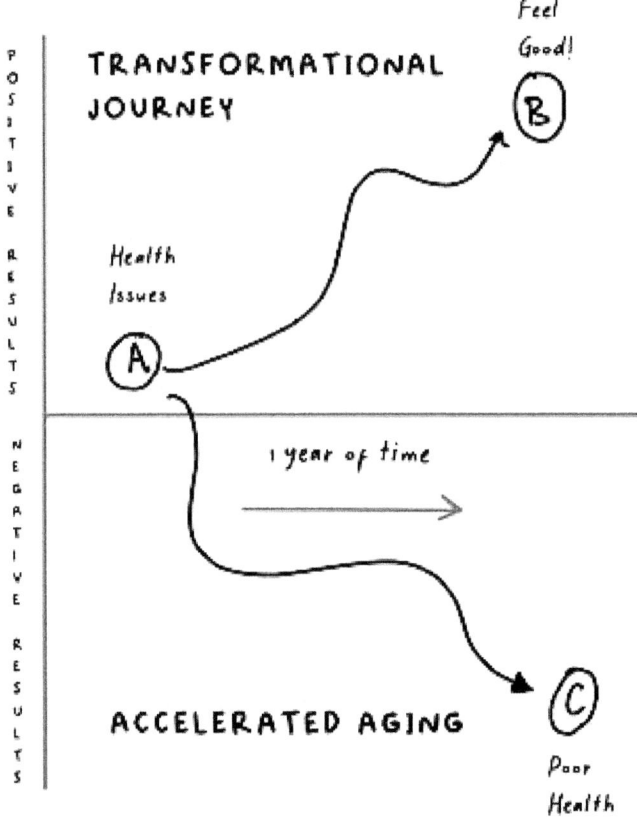

If you're afraid to talk about money, that is a hurdle you'll need to clear. You'll need sales training, role-playing, and having at least a few weekly sales conversations.

You'll need practice and continual improvement. When your goal becomes sales-generating activities... and you focus on leads and sales, you'll be able to sell out seats and create a waiting list.

Sales conversations happen one on one. While some people are hesitant to talk to people who can help them, others are not. For those who are reluctant to schedule a 1-1 complimentary session to discover their challenges and goals, you'll want to learn how to overcome their hesitation. Text messaging sometimes leads naturally to a zoom meeting or phone conversation. Even a hesitant person will schedule a conversation once you've earned their trust and they see the value in talking with you.

At Wellness Pro Academy, for conversations with prospects, we use Alex Hormozi's Closer Framework:

- C-larify why they are there
- L-abel the Problem
- O-verview of their past pain
- S-ell the VACATION
- E-xplain away the concern
- R-einforce their decision

We train our wellness pros to schedule sales conversations, track their scheduled conversations, and follow the framework. You'll want to be able to talk about YOUR CLUB OFFER if the prospect is a fit.

For CLUB THRIVE, we offer a Body Goals Session to see if CLUB THRIVE is a good fit for the prospect. In the session, we use the Closer Framework. Here are questions written as if "You" is your prospect."

C-LARIFY why they are there:

- What made you schedule?
- What compelled you to show up here today?
- What's your goal right now?
- Why is that important to you?
- What's not working?
- What's your goal? The challenge? Your timeline (by WHEN)?

L-ABEL the Problem:

- What are they struggling with? What's not working? Label the problem.
- Confirm you're on the same page.
- So, ____ x is the problem?
- Sum up their problems. Get confirmation (So, did we nail your problem?

O-VERVIEW of their past pain:

- What have you tried so far to fix it?
- How long did you do it for?
- How did that work for you?
- What else have you tried?
- What is it costing you? Asses a $ amount)
- When do you want to be at your goal? (explore one year)

TRANSITION POINT

If we think CLUB THRIVE will guide them to reach their goals, we ask permission to tell them about it. PAUSE to get invited to pitch.

S-ELL the VACATION:

- Find 2-3 features of your club that address their specific challenges. Use an analogy or story on why/how/by when you are going to be able to solve the problems you labeled in terms of desired result and timeline
- Analogy/End result 1
- Analogy/End result 2
- Analogy/End result 3
- Tell a past client or Club Member Success Story
- Do you want to do it? (PAUSE)
- The Offer: Briefly summarize why it's a year, how it works and the investment, and how it will save them money and time, and sell sell sell the vacation.

E-XPLAIN away the concern (OBJECTIONS)

- (VISION) If they don't know if your CLUB will work for them, return to sell the vacation - sell _the feeling of them accomplishing their goals_
- (LOGIC) If you work with us do you think you have a _greater or lower chance_ of resolving the problems (relist labeled problems)
- (DESIRE) Do you _want_ to work with me? If it were free, would you be all in?
- (FUN) Do you think it would be fun (name vibe) to be surrounded by a CLUB that was into result 1, result 2, result 3
- (INVEST) Do you believe it's worth investing in yourself to resolve the problems? Do you have access to funds or credit, or do you know someone who does?
- (CHOICE) Do you want to pay in 1 payment or spread the payments out over the first six months? You'll save money by paying in one payment.

R-EINFORCE their Decision:

People decide within the first 48 hours from the point of sale whether they will buy from you again. Use it to your advantage to create an excellent onboarding experience.

- Send a video message reinforcing their decision
- Mail them something to welcome them to your club

In the following sections, we'll examine money objections and how to find your future members.

Jane

Say, for instance, you determine your future member is a professional woman between 40-55 years old. Let's name her Jane. Jane earns over $80k per year. If she has a partner, the household income is over $150k. She is 15-50 pounds overweight. She feels like she is trading time for money. Her periods and perimenopausal symptoms are getting more challenging to manage. She has a hard time getting a good night's sleep. She has a gym membership. She likes hiking and yoga. Jane wishes she had a meditation practice to decrease her anxiety, but it never sticks. She eats out a few lunches and dinners out per week. Jane drinks at least a few bottles of wine per week. Her friendships are fun, but they aren't progressive. Jane enjoys a few vacations a year–to a tropical paradise or a ski trip. She always wishes she felt better in her bikini or ski pants.

In talking with Jane about what she most profoundly wants in life, she says: *I want to feel like I'm on top of my game. I want a raise. I know losing weight and getting better sleep would help me make that happen. I want more independence with my work. I want my salary and bonuses based on my performance. I want to feel in charge of my time and have more free time. I'm drinking too much wine, but it's hard to stop when my partner enjoys wine. I want to be on top of my game. I don't want to keep going in the direction I'm currently heading–more wine, more weight, and hitting my head on the glass ceiling. When I go on vacation, I want to look great, but most of all, I want to feel great in my body.*

You can use the Dan Sullivan question, *"Jane if we were having this conversation twelve months from today, and you were looking back at the past twelve months, what would have needed to happen for you to feel happy with your results?"*

Then you listen.
You listen hard.

You make sure you learn and reflect on all aspects of what winning looks like for Jane in 12 months. Take notes so you can be sure of where she is starting now (A) and where she wants to be (B) in her own words. Understand what is stopping her from getting there on her own.

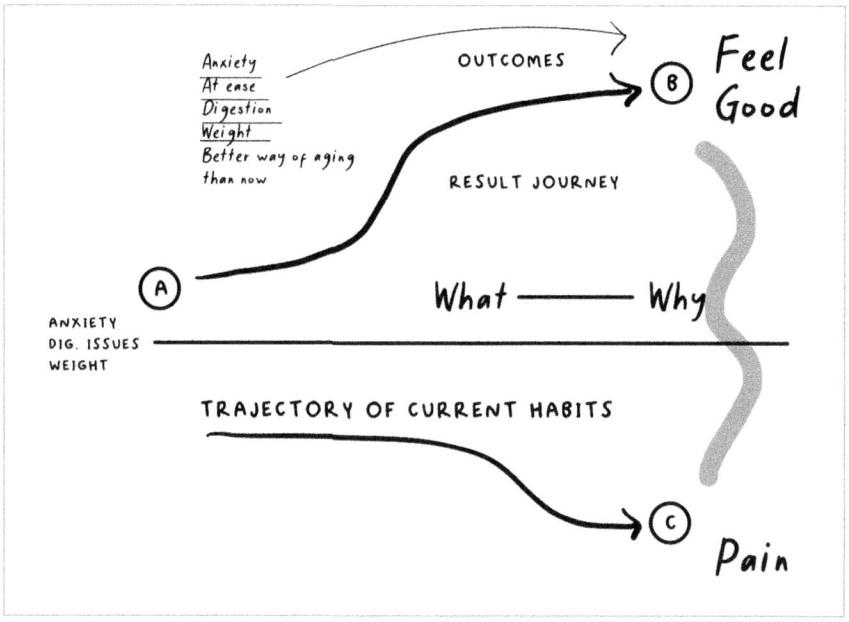

You label the problem, finding out what she has tried and what went sideways. Ask her if her partner has similar habits. Ask her if her friends or family have similar habits. Find out what worked in the past but didn't stick. Find out why Jane is stuck and how she has already identified what she needs to change.

At the transition, before selling the vacation, check in with your gut, with your heart.

Is Jane a good fit for your club? How, specifically, could your club solve her problems?

The big question is, do you believe you could get Jane to excellent results in one year? Remember how you would guide her over the year. Recall what is included in your package to get her results.

If so, the big question for Jane to make this massive leap in her life is, how tired is she of being stuck? Tired enough to invest in a new path for herself? Make sure Jane is aware she is making a choice. Either life is on top of her, or she is on top of life.

A choice must be made. Her old way of investing her money isn't getting her what she wants. Is she uncomfortable enough to change her pattern of investing?

If so, you can say something like, "Jane, based on what you've told me about how you're feeling, where you're stuck, and what you could reasonably do if you felt great, it sounds like we should get you on track to feeling great."

Ask her if she wants to hear how you could help her. Then, pause. She will say yes. Most people don't ask this question before presenting a solution. It's a crucial question. You want to be invited to share your solution rather than going into it uninvited.

If yes, tell her you'll be guiding a Body Wisdom Club—a breakthrough club, to have the best years of their life now. Tell her specifically in ways that relate to her current challenges. Ask her if she trusts you as a leader and participates wholeheartedly in your journey; what might she make happen? The tuition is $420 a month for 12 months. Directly ask her, "Does my Body Wisdom Club sound like an effective action plan to you?" If Jane says "Yes, " ask her if she is ready for you to guide her into feeling great.

Chances are, Jane will have objections; let's say it's a money objection. Not to worry, this is the process by which leads become members.

FIND THE MONEY

I've found most people don't know how to invest in their bodies.

By my mid-twenties, I was fortunate to discover the life-enhancing experience of investing in body wisdom. Year after year, I've heavily invested in training to learn holistic medicine to heal myself and experience body intelligence as I age.

The challenge is to calculate how much to invest, where best to invest, and the return on investment. Yet, we may find patterns if we look at case studies or citizen data.

As a citizen group, wellness pros have invested the most heavily, over time, in body wisdom. Most wellness pros start their wellness journey looking for help to heal themselves. As a progression from personal learning to professional training happens, more investment is made, which benefits the wellness pro in their body wisdom and earning potential. Many wellness pros prioritized wellness wisdom above working corporate or higher-paying jobs that wouldn't permit a wellness lifestyle. I know my story as a healer is common.

Yet, most of your future CLUB members have no idea how to invest in their bodies. What is covered by state or private health insurance is sick-care. The prospect must be educated to invest, out of pocket, in the future if they want to experience body wisdom.

Wellness pros, that is *your* job.

Your job is to guide your future club members in investing in the future body they want to experience.

As you get good at sales, objections, especially about money, are invitations to dive deep into the future your prospect wants to experience and explain away their concerns. Here are two questions:

1. Does your prospect think your club will get them to their goals?
2. Does your prospect think your club is a good investment?

To become a member of your club, they are fundamentally changing how they invest.

You can not underestimate the power of getting good at helping people invest in what they want. It's not intuitive. Often, your prospect will also need to communicate their investment decisions to a partner, and their decision will be a change from the values they were raised with or taught.

The money to invest in the future body they want to experience is either being misallocated or tied up in investments that don't improve their day-to-day quality of life.

So where is the money going to come from? There is a yoga story of a student asking a master the same question. They wanted to build a bigger center to serve more people. "Where is the money going to come from," the student asked. The master responded, "From wherever it is right now."

So, where is the money right now... becomes the question you want to think long and hard about. Right now, people want to feel better. But, often, they haven't thought through where the money will come from to invest in what they want.

For your future members to invest in your club, you will need to change some of their beliefs. This is the part of your wellness business called marketing and sales.

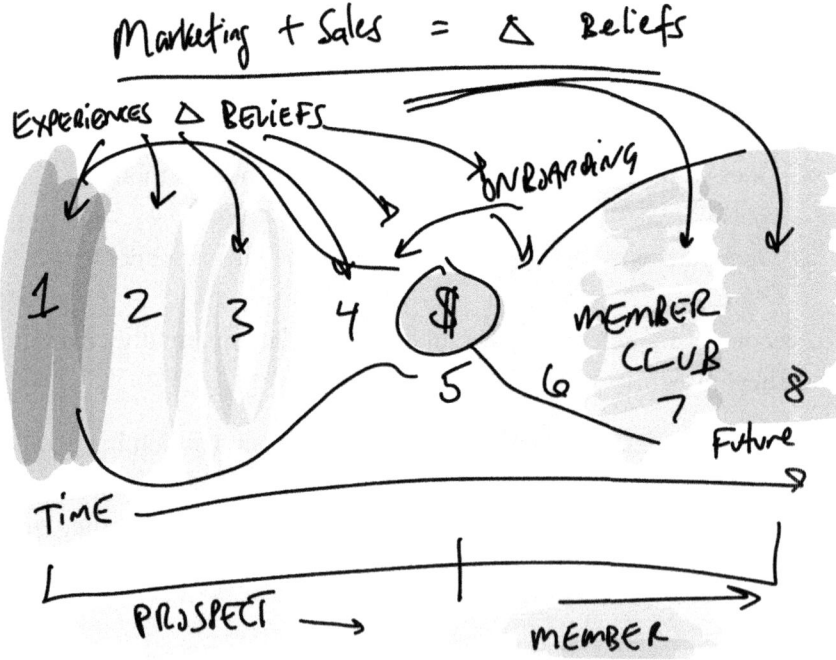

One way to change beliefs is to show your future member where they are wasting that $5000 and not earning a return on that investment.

That $5000 could be going down the drain. That $5000 may even be spent on stuff that reinforces their symptoms.

Find the Money for Career Professionals

One of my favorite exercises is finding out the cost of symptoms. Because most people you'll talk to have symptoms of chronic inflammation physically and emotionally, this can help a club prospect evaluate how to invest in their future. (See Appendix on Reversing Chronic Inflammation).

This is a reallocation exercise. You are looking for where the money is currently going. First, look for costs that feed inflammation–like eating out, convenience foods, and alcohol. Next, look for expenses that result from the inflammation - like income plateauing, supplements, and retail therapy. You can also look for high-cost items with a low return on their end goals, like expensive vacations or a new car.

Say for Jane, you go through the costs and discover:

- Food Waste & Eating Out: $2400/year
- Tropical Trip: $5000/year
- Wine: $500/year
- Supplements: $500/year
- Income Plateau: $4000/year ($40k for ten years)

COST OF INFLAMMATION

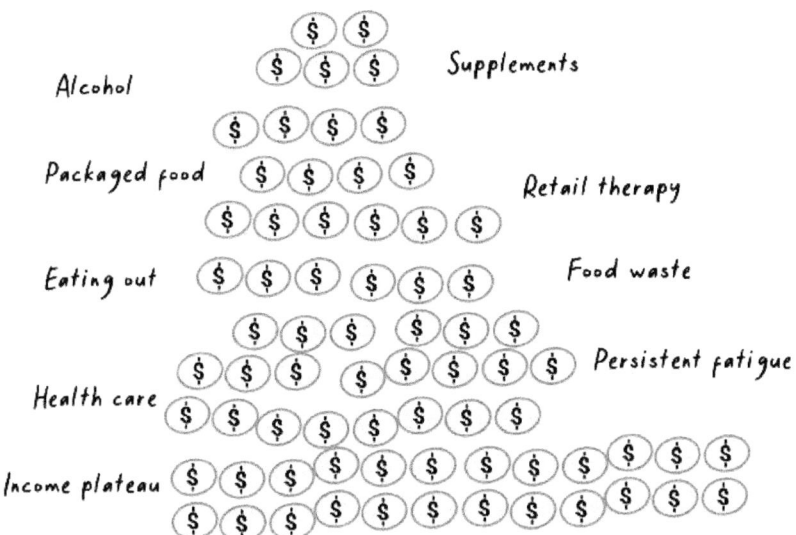

As you see above, the highest cost for Jane is the opportunity cost of income plateau. This is common with chronic inflammation due to fatigue and the lack of focus and ambition that accompanies systemic inflammation.

A previous study found that a heavy woman will earn $9,000 less annually than an average-weight woman of the same skill, education and work experience. A very heavy woman will pay a penalty of almost $19,000 annually.[1]

To recap, Jane isn't confident in her body. She isn't getting good sleep. She doesn't seem to be performing as well at work. Because she is a career professional, she has an opportunity in the marketplace to earn higher performance pay, year over year. A 5% raise at her $80000 a year job is $4000.

Suppose she were to wake up to her potential, dial in her body rhythms, arrive at her optimal weight, and automate healthier habits. In that case, it's reasonable to believe she could increase her salary by $20,000 a year over the next few years. There are plenty of examples of this happening annually in every industry and economy. Being on top of your game and becoming increasingly useful in whatever is currently happening earns rewards in the professional marketplace. If Jane is under-slept and bloated with sugar from wine, you'll miss growth opportunities daily.

Look to your past clients to witness the reality of this opportunity cost. As you empower people by empowering their habits, their opportunities take on a much better trajectory.

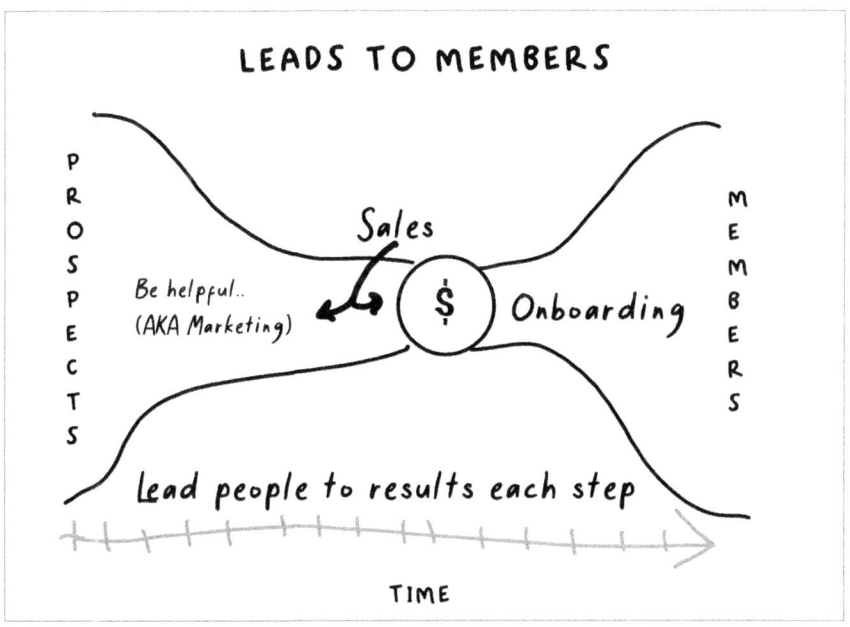

Find the Money for People with Investments

Many of your club prospects have invested in their home and retirement funds. Often there is a disconnect around investing in what they want to experience in their body and their health declines with age. They are trained to feel secure by seeing a number on a screen, for example, the Dow Jones index. When a prospect works with me in CLUB THRIVE, they say it was the best investment of their life.

But that doesn't mean it was easy to reallocate funds from an investment source and into their body. How to quantify what their quality of life and their future experience is worth is not how people today are trained to think.

Their biggest hurdle isn't the money... it's how your prospects think about investing.

We've worked with many wellness pros who were uncomfortable discussing money with their prospects. We help wellness pros change their perspective to see the investment conversation as a service. Guide your prospect to understand how people who invest in themselves make decisions. You are helping your prospect address how to invest as their core obstacle to feeling better. Now, they have a chance to feel better in their future.

For example, most wellness pros invest at least $5000 in their wellness wisdom per year, above their non-wellness colleagues, in trainings, mentoring, wellness retreats, and detoxes. Wellness pros spend more on supplements and organic foods. And they wouldn't trade *feeling better* for other investments.

> Despite 66% of global consumers feeling financially squeezed, 80% said they plan to maintain or increase spending related to health and fitness (both products and services) in the next year. (Source: Accenture)
>
> Accenture's Consumer Pulse Survey 2022

They need to evaluate the return on investing in their body. And you'll have to break it down into dollars and sense. You'll want to revisit Label the Problem in Hormozi's framework and get dollar values on their problem.

For example,

- What is worth playing tennis (or another mobility activity worth a year?
- What is playing with their grandkids worth a year?
- What is being attractive worth a year?

Identify the beliefs that need changing and the spending/investing patterns under them. Once you have done this, you can use your process to help people become leads.

---

1. https://www.forbes.com/sites/lisaquast/2011/06/06/can-being-thin-actually-translate-into-a-bigger-paycheck-for-women/?sh=3dbb43a57b03

TO FIND YOUR MEMBERS, FIND YOUR HUBS

> The best form of marketing is the kind of marketing you will actually do.
>
> Tad Hargrave, Marketing for Hippies, Hub Marketing Ebook

Just to be crystal clear, you have a new problem. Now that you know who Jane is, the next question is, where do you find 20 Jane's? If you want 20 people in your club this year, the leering question is, where are the 20 people right now who need you to guide them on this unique unicorn of a transformational CLUB?

Where is *Jane* already looking for you? That is where *you* go to find Jane.

The Janes of the world need your help finding you. Who does Jane trust? Where is she looking for information? Who does Jane listen to? You don't wait for your people to find your club.

With Hub Marketing - you go to the hubs where your Jane's already are. I interviewed Tad Hargrave of Marketing for Hippies, who wrote the book on HUB Marketing. In this section, I've pulled out the core concepts for you.

Tad insists that for wellness pros in our situation - looking for our club members - we connect with hubs, who can share about us through word of mouth.

Word of Mouth

In your world, who are the talkers? Who is in the know? Who is the connoisseur of experiences? Who has a credible reputation? Who is a reliable source of information?

You might reflect, "I am." And that is true. You are a hub. Tad points out that if you are an Active Hub, you're actively looking to be a better connector for your community.

Hubs connect to other hubs. You're looking to connect to people who are already connected to your Janes and might want to cross-promote or be helpful to their hub by knowing about your CLUB.

Who comes to mind?

Ask yourself, where does Jane spend time? Chances are, Jane follows people on Facebook and Instagram. As a professional, Jane is also on LinkedIn. Jane sees a doctor annually who makes holistic wellness referrals. Jane's company also offers lunch and learns, where people can give free talks. Jane's gym also offers spaces to teach workshops. These are different categories of hubs.

Tad lists out seven categories of Hubs:

Hubs by Category

1. EVENTS and LOCATIONS: Where does Jane gather, congregate, celebrate and hang out?
2. BUSINESSES: Where does Jane already spend her money?
3. GROUPS: What groups is she a part of?
4. SUPPORT: What resources or groups exist to support her?
5. PUBLICATIONS (print and web): Where does Jane go for news and information that is relevant, credible, and valuable to her?
6. INDIVIDUALS: Who does she most trust (whether globally or locally)?
7. WEB SEARCH: if Jane searched for a solution to a problem on Google, what would she type in?

Go through each of the categories to answer the question. Use a google doc so you can build a plan off of this. We'll help you develop the plan into action in Wellness Pro Academy. Look for hubs that are well respected, well connected, and open to endorsing what they like. Choose hubs with similar convictions and a compatible vibe.

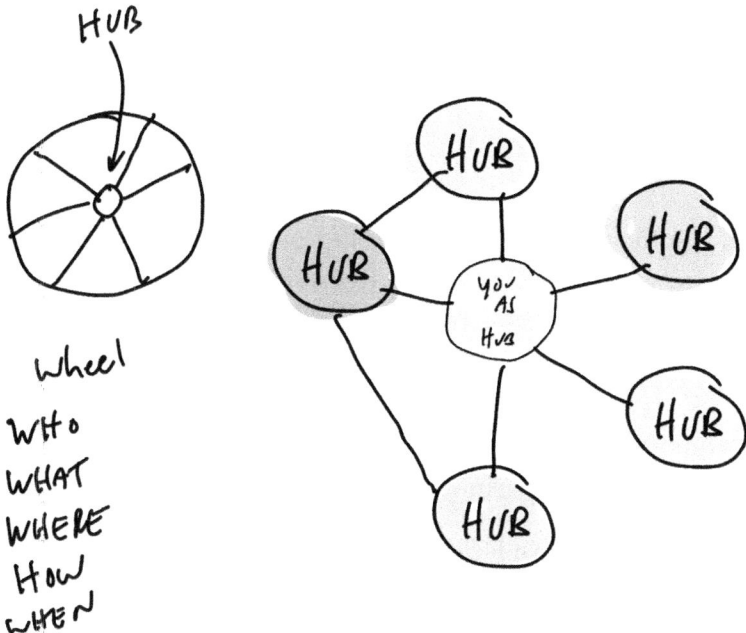

One Hub a Week

Now, Tad recommends connecting with a new hub once a week. Reach out to learn more about what they do, who they serve, and if they are interested in exploring collaborations or what else might be possible. Then, when you meet, find out what they specialize in, what their favorite clients or customers are interested in, and what is coming up next for them.

Before you leave the conversation, find out who else they know that you should talk to.

If your hub and you decide to collaborate, Tad has the best advice in his ebook on Hub Marketing:

If you are approaching someone, the central question in your mind must be, "How can I make this all as clear, quick, easy and worthwhile for them as possible?" You're in their house. You are a guest. Don't waste their time.

Tad Hargrave

When I started my business in San Francisco in 2001, I went to yoga studios and asked if I could teach a free or paid workshop on Ayurveda. All of my first clients came from intro to Ayurveda workshops. When I moved back to Idaho (for the skiing!) I took the same approach but expanded regionally from Sun Valley to Jackson Hole. I also looked for events and venues where my Jane's were buying vegetables and supplements, and getting information from, like wellness festivals.

You can become known locally by doing pop-up events at yoga studios, holistic health clinics, and even health food stores. When you work with a hub, your job is to make everything easy for them to share what is worth sharing with their people.

Free Talks

A straightforward way to generate roughly five leads per month is to have one free talk or pop-up event, including a 1-1 Body Goals Session with you, before or after the event. With five leads per month, you should easily enroll almost two people per month. Bam. You will have the best work of your life helping your 20 Janes and a lucrative lifestyle.

Here is how it works for Erica, a Wellness Pro Academy member, "Literally every free talk or referral goes straight into a strategy session (in a loving, receiving, open-hearted way). I have three sales calls this week, that are as far as I can tell, largely "yes." All think my offer is super reasonable. My point is that I've never focused on sales being #1, but thanks to Wellness Pro Academy, even amid the chaos, my dreams of a lucrative practice are coming real! And my sales skills, which were previously non-existent, seem to be improving!"

Where do you need to start?

Andy Sernovitz of Word of Mouth Marketing breaks word of mouth marketing into five easy steps:

1. Find the right people to talk about you (hubs)
2. Give them something to talk about (be useful and make them look good to their people)
3. Create tools to make it easier for them to spread the word (ex. how-to videos, tip sheets, infographics, playlists)
4. Participate in the conversation
5. Track and measure the results

Put your sweat equity into word of mouth and referrals from hubs. Here are examples of tools to make for your hubs. You could make an online quiz for hubs to share. For example, "Is your health in the way of your next raise?" take the quiz. You could do a free talk or make a tip sheet on "How to Get a Better Night Sleep to Feel Light + Look Great." You could do this locally, at the gym, women's health center, a regional wellness festival, a corporate supplement company lunch and learn, or yoga studio.

Remember, people want to feel better.

Your future members are looking for a breakthrough. Your power to find your 20 Janes is determined by how much responsibility you will assume in finding her. Assume your responsibility is to find her and align your actions accordingly. She exists and needs you to find her.

Marketing is how you uplevel your prospect's experiences and beliefs.

Review your CONVICTIONS. Who needs to hear them? People looking for a solution to their problems will notice you. With conviction, you articulate the highest value you can provide. If you stand by your convictions and offer what your people need - transformational results - you can scale your wellness business.

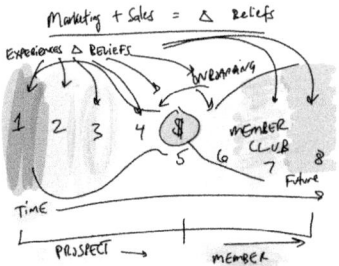

If you do, you'll scale your wellness business.

TRANSFORMATION

Guided Transformation holds the highest value traded in today's marketplace.

Guided transformation has been the pinnacle of the global economy throughout history. Remember this when wondering the best way to use your wellness skills. You'll start seeing your market position from a sharper angle. So, what is guided transformation?

Think about your healing journey. Who were your guides? Did you have a teacher? A mentor? A healer? Make a quick list right now. Then, write beside each name how much you invested in each training or relationship.

Now, make a second list.

List anyone who guided your transformation into becoming a wellness pro. Your teachers, your mentors. The licenses and certifications you earned.

How much did you invest in becoming the wellness pro you are today? Be precise in your re-accounting of your financial and time investment. If you traveled to learn, include that.

I moved across two states to study for two years, to learn and earn two distinct certifications. Once I had my credentials, I went to India to study with two additional gurus or masters. When I returned to the US, I found two more teachers, one for advanced yoga training and another for enlightenment and advanced meditation training. Over the years, I've invested $50,000 in wellness pro skills. For business skills, I've invested another $80,000. This doesn't include other skills from my undergraduate degree in International Relations and Environmental Politics. All these investments transformed me into the healer, coach, and business owner I am today. (The undergraduate degree gave me skills in research and writing that helped me write books).

The return on these investments has been 2000%, so I continue investing more. Remember–it's not the spending that matters ... it's the investing for a return on investment that predicates success. Growth experiences with exceptional guides are the bulk of how I invest in myself. I'm not unusual.

Whatever your investments total, honor the transformation that upleveled you in the process.

Now, back to you. Who are your top three to five guides you've invested the most money with? Look at your notes. You wouldn't know what you know now without that person guiding you to a higher level of understanding. You wouldn't be who you are today without having had that experience.

Now, take a moment and pause. Reflect. Feel gratitude for these guides in your body. Bow to your best guides for how they helped you develop personally and professionally based on their wisdom and experiences.

I hope a lightbulb in your head is turning on. You get to deliver more value. And, you get to receive exponentially more money for your effectiveness in guiding your people and your clients through a powerful, invested transformational journey. You'll bring the best you have to the table. For how we reverse the symptoms of chronic inflammation in CLUB THRIVE- see the Appendix on Reversing Chronic Inflammation.

You will evolve *with* your club. You will lead by improving your club's transformational experience for your current and future members. You will innovate as you learn and nurture a unique journey that only you can design and deliver. You get to design this remarkable journey for precisely who you can best help. You get to make it even better than you experienced in your journey to thrive.

You get to make it better, to improve upon it, to innovate a unique journey that only you could design and deliver.

Remember how the top right part of the economic value ladder goes to premium and differentiation? What differentiates you from other wellness pros becomes your differentiation in the marketplace. At the level of transformational experience, you have no competitors. No one can compete because no one will design this transformational CLUB as you will. What makes you different is now your best advantage.

Because you get to charge a premium at this level, you don't need to work with many people. Exclusivity is built in. Inclusivity is also built-in for your members. I'll get deep into premium pricing in the next part, so if you've undervalued your services–stay tuned.

Many wellness pros want to know how to serve the masses and earn more. The way to do that is to have free and paid versions. My free version is my podcast and free workshops. That drives people who want to join my club closer to me while educating the masses for free.

If you want to earn more and don't have a higher price point transformational CLUB to guide your people to a better reality, you're doing something wrong. You are making it impossible to earn at a higher level with more specific and better results. That is the beauty of truly understanding and embracing the Value of Economic Progression.

What does this look like? When you lead a transformational CLUB that people want to be part of, you can charge what the transformation is worth.

A good starting price point is about $5000 with 20 people, so we'll use that as an example. Here is a snapshot of what this might look like, enrolling members quarter by quarter throughout the year. The rest of this book unpacks how to do just this.

ANNUAL INCOME: 100K

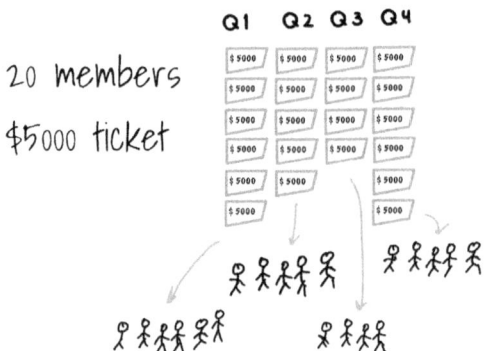

Once you get this, a few issues or hurdles are essential to build new skills and behaviors to bust your glass ceiling. Let's tackle this one by one, so you can earn more faster! The first is your convictions about wellness habits, the second is your CLUB structure, and the third is sales and marketing skills. The good news is that there is an easy way over all three hurdles!

The wild thing about leading a CLUB to results... is that your CLUB turns around and leads you.

When you lead a community, the community starts to develop the leader within you. A leadership circle within your club develops and moves forward when you lead.. and listen.

I've been guiding transformation for twenty years. Leading members to results made me wealthy while making me into the leader I'm meant to be. I've seen this time and again with this smarter CLUB model.

Building a club to guide a transformation creates the container, structure, or wall, separating members from non-members, the committed from the non-committed, and the non-invested. Containers are crucial for providing structure to enable personal and collective evolutions.

In LEAD YOUR CLUB (Use PROMO code: PRO497 to get in free), you'll schedule a 1-1 wellness career coaching session so we can help you with these hurdles. We'll guide you to clarify your potential Club, built from your unique convictions, mission, training, and ambition.

SUCCESS

IMPOSTER SYNDROME

At this point, the elephant in the room for any wellness pro usually is their habit integrity.

Modern life is full of stressors that bring us away from the natural rhythm of early to bed, early to rise. Everyday life is increasingly digital– escorting us away from unadulterated experiences of nature. Being in nature restores us.

Sometimes wellness pros have what is called "imposter syndrome." Imposter syndrome is where you feel like you are an imposter rather than the real deal. With circadian rhythm habits, almost every modern wellness pro I meet feels like an imposter ... one who may know which habits are better for them but cannot commit to better habits in their busy life.

Now, you don't need to guide yourself and your members to have these habits perfectly dialed in all the time. At Wellness Pro Academy, we erase imposter syndrome with essential habits. We cultivate a culture of integrity with the proven habits that work for humans - the habits of the circadian rhythm.

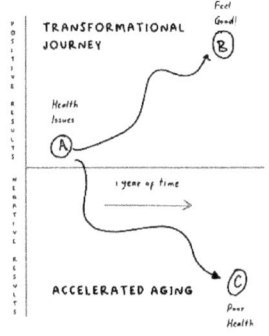

Which circadian rhythm habits lead one out of health issues into feeling good? If you've ever gone camping without your electronics, you might have noticed that you got sleepy earlier. Did you sleep more? Did you enjoy the stars? Did you feel the breeze? Nature restores us into rhythm.

The Essential Habits of Wellness Pros:

1. Eat an earlier, lighter dinner to reduce digestive pressure on the body
2. Enjoy your evening offline, and go to bed early
3. Wake early, hydrate, eliminate your bowels
4. Do breathing and movement before the day begins
5. Intermittent fast, for your body type
6. Make your seasonal food fresh and daily from whole local foods
7. Attune your senses to nature
8. Meditate, reflect, or sit in silence to clear your mind

You need enough of the habits enough of the time. We aim for a solid B-, not a perfect A+. Your body can then clean up any chronic inflammation and restore a high-level quality to your systems and tissues.

As a modern wellness pro, you may also have chronic systemic inflammation or a degenerative disease. It's not too late to start feeling better. You'll be both a member and the leader of your club, leading with integrity, approachability, and vulnerability. And, not to worry– we also train wellness pros to guide themselves and their members out of the pain cave of chronic inflammation.

TARGET

It's better to hang out with people better than you. Pick out associates whose behavior is better than yours, and you'll drift in that direction.[1]

Warren Buffett

To Warren Buffett's point—you've been hanging out with me reading this book. I hope by now, the possibility of you leading a transformational journey and earning based on results is top of mind for you. Leave this book with a specific goal and a discipline to that goal.

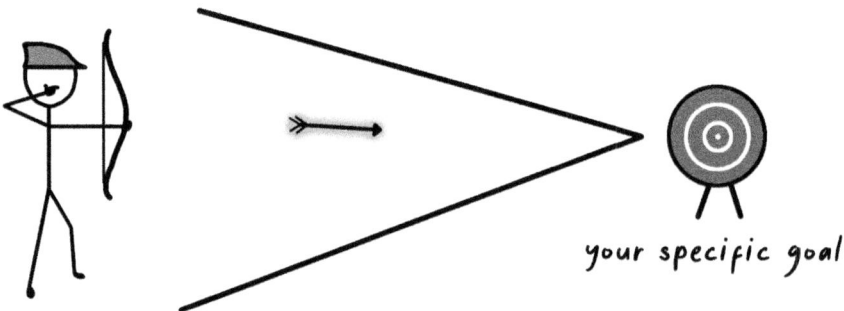

your specific goal

I have four essential questions for you to identify your goal and further drift in this direction. There are no right or wrong answers. There are your inner truths. Wrap up this process by summarizing what you discovered in this book:

1. How badly do you want to lead people to feel good?
2. What experiences and habits would you design into your CLUB?
3. How much money do you want to make annually, and how much time do you want to work weekly?
4. What would you do with more money and more time?

If you don't take the time to answer the four questions above, pitfalls will arise. The first pitfall is you won't know what is at stake. If you aren't honest with yourself about what is at stake, you won't change. Is that worth $15k? $50k? $100k? $250k? Only you can invest in yourself.

The second pitfall is that you won't clarify or articulate your ambition to help people with what you know. To me, your ambition is sacred. What you most deeply want is as close to a divine directive as it gets.

Your focus determines your reality.

Qui-Gon Jinn, Star Wars

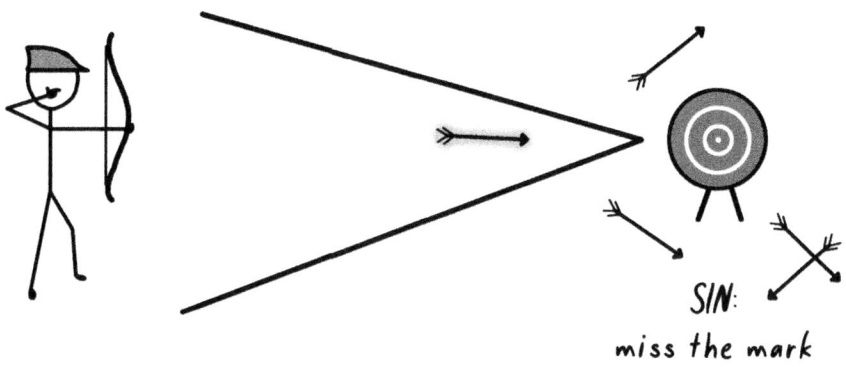

SIN:
miss the mark

If you don't clarify your true ambitions, you'll miss the mark on your life. You'll sacrifice your greatness, which gives your life meaning. Your ambition is sacred. Honor your ambition. Protect it. Serve it.

I watched many seasoned wellness pros give up on their true ambitions. Ambitions of impact. Ambitions of financial savings. Ambitions of a particular lifestyle. Ambition to go deeper into wisdom. Ambitions of leadership.

I want to leave you with the singular potential within you and your membership club. I'll share an image below from mapping out the Wellness Pro Academy member JC's club culture. JC was clear that the club culture she would create for her members would balance her intensity to be all in and do hard things with experiencing support and bonding while learning Ayurveda.

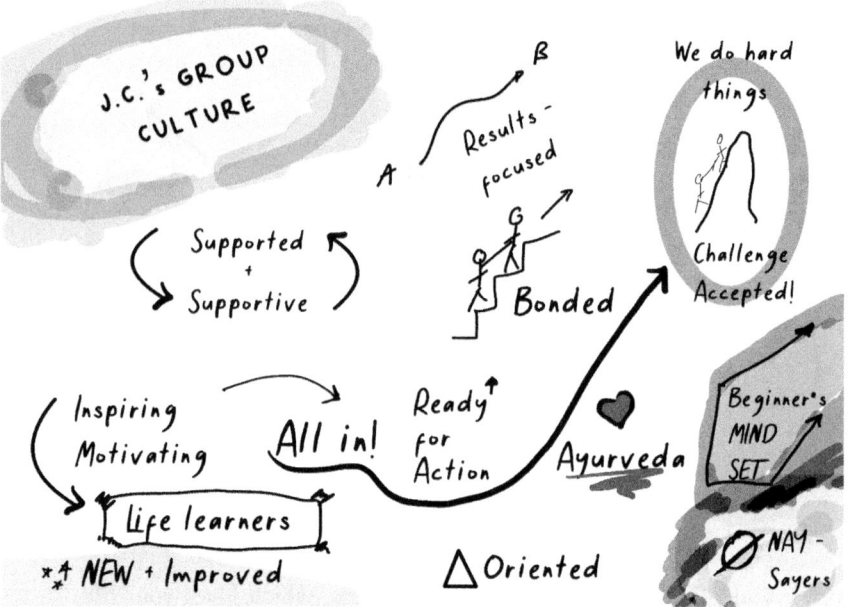

This is the process of making your members' journey real. You create what you think would be the best experience ever. Then, you get to test it. You'll improve it in motion as you enroll your next quarter. This is the earn while you learn.

I guided JC to vision her club with her club culture. Her ambition sparked. She could see her purpose. Her purpose was to provide a unique club with a life-changing experience. She saw how this would evolve her personality as a leader. She could see how her habits, in how she would run her career, would need to evolve radically. And she was up for the challenge.

JC also realized that this is how it would be for her members. She would guide her members to be clear on their purpose. She could support and bond her members on a challenging journey to explore their dharma (purpose). She would rely on her background in yoga and Ayurveda.

She knew this was a call to do the most important work of her life.

You'll be happiest and most helpful when you do your best work by guiding the most profound transformation when your members have skin in the game for you to earn and lead well. When you can guide people to get what they want faster, you dramatically alter the trajectory of their lives ... and yours.

To make this book work for you, ascertain what you need to do to make this happen. Here are my final questions for you to answer:

- What are you going to need to know that you don't know? (Ex.sales generating activities)
- Where are you going to be challenged? (Ex. Generating leads, giving free talks, sales conversations, closing)
- Where have you stopped before? (Ex. Raising my rates, building a package, sales)
- Where are you going to stop? (Be honest. If you won't invest in sales training or training like the Wellness Pro Academy in how to do this method, then acknowledge that.)

In this book, I've covered why good habits matter for your clients, why you guide a unique club, how to build and price your club offer, why your future members will pay a premium for the results to be guided by you, and how to attract your future members.

In all the work I've done guiding wellness pros to a more successful career, I've found that if you want to help people, there are plenty of people who need help. Focus on being helpful. Commit to leading results to the transformational journey.

Use this method to up your game. Confront your demons along the way, and get on to the best work of your life.

1. https://www.thegentlemansjournal.com/what-warren-buffett-wants-you-to-invest-in/#:

INVESTED

Your greatness is limited only by the investments you make in yourself.

Grant Cardone, Sales Entrepreneur Billionaire

The more developed we become as individuals, the more we are willing to pay for exactly what we want, coaching and information, and we buy less stuff. Reflect on how you spend. Reflect on how you invest. Reflect on which of your investments, including investments in growing your wisdom, have the best return on investment (ROI).

Look at spending versus investing with business training for entrepreneurs and the self-employed. Like all entrepreneurs, wellness pros are self-employed or employed by their businesses. When you work for yourself and want to grow your income, you need entrepreneurial and business training, like all other entrepreneurs in the marketplace.

Business training is different than service or modality training. Investing in modality training is essential to get the skills to do the service, ex—teaching yoga as a service you offer. To get your company of one to grow, pay your bills, and increase your investments, you need modality (think services) *and* business training.

Some entrepreneurs and wellness pros view their service training and business training as an expense. Yet, successful entrepreneurs view training as an investment. They expect a high return on that investment. Why? Because business training requires their full attention, which means it'll require both a time investment and financial investment on their part.

For the wellness pros who join me for guidance in leading the journey—who enroll in the Wellness Pro Academy –there are a few skills gaps. The reason they invest is to close those gaps fast and get on to earning more by doing the best work of their lives. When they close those gaps the immediate effect is a return on their tuition investment with me.

What are the gaps?
Offer.
Sales.
Leads.
Dynamic club leadership.

The second income-multiplying investment obstacle for wellness pros is differentiating business training from service training. We've found wellness pros more easily recognize the value, for example, in an Advanced Yoga Therapeutics training, or a Yoga Philosophy Training, than in a training to grow their business. This perspective on investment becomes a stumbling block for most wellness pros desiring to reach higher planes of financial and career success.

At the Wellness Pro Academy, we train wellness professionals to uplevel living their wellness wisdom to serve at their next level of impact with ease. We consistently find the wellness pros who come to us, having previously invested in business training are the most growth-oriented. Their prior investments in business smarts and service smarts are earning them a better return, which sets them up for better opportunities.

If you're good at what you do, and you have the right business model and training, the sky is the limit. In the Wellness Pro Academy, we guide the business model of leading the journey, including the sales and marketing necessary to sell out seats. We guide you in how to lead your club, how to lead yourself in integrity with your wellness lifestyle, and how to earn through providing deeper value. Many of our Wellness Pro Academy members get up and running in their first six months with us in this model, which could earn them double in half the time with committed, results-invested clients. Our members report the program is an investment with an exponential ROI.

If you want to be financially successful as a wellness pro, don't view your career training as an expense. Put your money or earned good credit to the highest return on investment. That is the best place for anyone to put their money. If that investment is you because you're self-employed, you have an exponential potential or exponential ROI.

The way I think of it is the more value I can offer them more I should be paid. My focus is on adding value to the market. Right now, my job as leader of WELLNESS PRO ACADEMY and CLUB THRIVE is to nurture a global community for people to thrive in their bodies, lives, and ecosystems. I write. I speak. I interview. I teach. I coach. Overall, I lead via the CLUB model structures.

The more I invest in on-the-job skills, the more successful I'll be at my job. I orient towards the next skills I need to be more effective in adding value by leading the CLUB for our global member community. The better I get at leading the transformational journey - paid members - and leading the global tribe with my vision, message, and teaching, the better I get at my job. The more money rolls in the door, the more adaptable my skills are for an unknown future.

(Note: many wellness pros at Wellness Pro Academy choose to lead small, local clubs. The CLUB model works great for those that want a hobby business or side hustle with their wellness wisdom.)

My members invest in themselves through me. Yours will invest in themselves through you. My members invest in my leadership and step-by-step guidance in their lives. Members' return on investment is exponential because their potential is ignited and in action.

You could do the same. The six to seven-figure business model requires your leadership. Lead the transformational CLUB. You'll have better integrity with your transformation and a leverageable business model to boot. Not bad.

I've found through over a decade of testing that guiding your people through a one-year transformational experience is the best way to lead to results. You'll both need to be committed, invested, and results-focused.

Sometimes, it doesn't seem like humans value transformation above all else, which means the modern marketplace has plenty of room for you to enter the picture. Most people don't know this transformational experience is possible for them. You, the leader, represent the results. Focus on guiding your people to whatever results you are embodying.

If you obsess about creating the most effective club, original to you,... you get to do the most gratifying work of your life. You get to earn as much as you want... because the model is based on results, scarcity (you can't lead that many people, after all), and leadership. You get to design your life according to desired results. Win. Win. Win.

Here is the link to apply for the Wellness Pro Academy.

APPENDIX on REVERSING CHRONIC INFLAMMATION

I've included chapters from Uninflamed. References to other chapters in UNINFLAMED appear in parenthesis. For example: (see HEAL).

UNINFLAMED (2022) 21 Anti-Inflammatory PRIMAL HABITS to Heal, Sleep better, Intermittent fast, Detox, Lose weight, Feel great, & Crush your life goals with a Kickass Microbiome

Check Your Symptoms

These are all symptoms of inflammation. If you have a lot, fear not! I'll walk you step by step through the habits that heal inflammation.

- Chronic low-grade stress, anxiety
- Depression, hopelessness, feeling trapped
- Irritability, frustration
- Overwhelm
- Brain fog, mental confusion, poor memory
- Difficulty making decisions, concentrating or focusing
- Poor willpower, unmotivated, low ambition

- Fatigue
- Poor sleep
- Joint pain, stiffness upon rising
- Feeling heavy, stagnant, stuck
- Poor digestion: bloating, irregular or loose stools, constipation, indigestion, bad breath, coated tongue
- Puffiness, water retention, sinus congestion
- Belly fat, cellulite, man boobs, spare tires, excess body weight

- Emotional eating: cravings for crappy foods, overeating
- Skin issues: rashes, hives, acne, psoriasis, eczema
- Allergies or asthma
- PMS, fibrocystic breasts, hard periods
- Headaches
- Susceptibility to illness, infection, or fungus
- High blood pressure
- Lack of sex drive

- Disconnect from purpose in daily life
- Unclear about purpose, direction, or strategy
- Lack of creativity and unique expression

Habits and the Human Potential

Lest we forget, our human biochemistry is subtle and sacred.

Humans orient towards purpose. We comprehend morality, we ritualize mortality. Humans dance; we sing, bike, ski, flip, fly. Humans hunt, build, make art, design, invent—create. Humans developed language to communicate ideas. We philosophize to reveal universal truths. We do math, physics, chemistry. We gather. We trade. We form teams, competing for fun and for growth. We collaborate globally via technology and telepathy.

Lest we forget, human beings are exquisitely designed, from physiology to psychology, to thrive in our communal society. The human biochemistry, our hardware and software, evolved with our universe, our planet, our biosphere—our collaborative home.

Yet, we have a problem.

The habits of modern humans are conventional to the point of poisoning people slowly into anxiety, depression, confusion and chronic disease. Children today are being born with preventable disease markers.

The good news? The conventional habits dehumanizing us are very new. They've only been around for a few generations. That means we can turn things around. *You* can turn things around.

The most serious and far-reaching result of our current habits—how we grow food, how frequently we eat, our chronic mental stress, the medicines we trust in, what we do each day without thinking—is that they are causing INFLAMMATION on a mass scale. Inflammation is the cause of most of today's symptoms and diseases in our bodies and minds.

But we can reverse it. We can change, we can move from our current sub-par experience to the state of "thrive," of being UN-INFLAMED. Hence the title of this book.

I will show you how. This book will take you through the best habits to turn things around. A lot of what I will show you is ancient wisdom, rediscovered, confirmed and supported by the latest scientific research. With true wisdom, you can move from the "now" of symptoms to a new "now" of thriving in your body, with a focused mind and aligned purpose for the next chapter of your life.

This is reality now.

With inflammation, we lose.

We lose feeling great in our wisdom years.

We lose the ability to focus our life towards meaning and purpose.

We lose the ease of relaxation.

We lose simple pleasures.

And, yet... problems are potentials.

I'll guide you through the habits that eat inflammation for breakfast, so you can reverse the damage caused by conventional habits. As you run experiments with the primal habits explored in this book, you'll recover your natural rhythm, befriend your body type, and feed your microbiome to optimize your genetics. Rhythm isn't a race against time.

You'll get leaner, stronger, smarter. With primal habits, you clear pain. You become the visionary; you learn who you will become next. You end up with more time, more money, less waste.

———

Your past determines your present.

Primal habits ignite your potential.

Potential churns critical issues to the surface. Embedded within problems are innovative solutions. The complexities of health issues mask the simplest solutions.

The primal habits have been cultured out of us.

Our potential—each and every one of us—is to culture for ourselves, once we have the knowledge, the habits that invigorate personal health and activate our collective intelligence.

You are a highly adaptable organism, designed to collaborate with potentiality. Remembering the primal habits will help you along the path to becoming who you always knew you were—and who you could become next.

Vital, awake, uninflamed... human.

The Problem

As a species, we've traded our primal ways and habits for convenience and comfort, and in return we've bought ourselves chronic disease.

If your symptoms are chronic, it feels like life is on top of you, rather than you being on top of life.

Inflammation is diagnosable as "chronic" if symptoms haven't abated within a year, if they limit your daily activities, or require ongoing medical attention. Humans naturally think in terms of years. You'll see me use images in the book to show you what can happen in a year. I'll show two trajectories: A to B for better health; A to C for chronic inflammation.

Before we continue, it's helpful to know the most common diseases and symptoms caused by inflammation.

IS INFLAMMATION CHRONIC? THE SYMPTOMS

- Waking up with stiff joints, a heavy mood, or puffy face
- Low energy, fatigue, insomnia
- Depression, anxiety, mood disorders
- Increasing sensitivities showing up as allergies: food allergies, asthma, skin issues (such as eczema or acne)
- Gastrointestinal issues, like constipation, diarrhea, acid reflux
- Weight creep
- Getting sick often
- Intense symptoms with viral infections, such as shingles, coronavirus, mononucleosis, pneumonia

Inflammation is often both a cause and result of stress. Stress on your body stresses out your microbiome—the community of microbes your cells depend on to function (see MICROBIOME). Stress on the mind is felt as adrenaline addiction, information overload, not enough sleep, not enough time or money, too few dynamic relationships. And, even if you're not overweight, chronic inflammation may compromise your immune system.

Inflammation makes it harder to do the right thing, the hard thing, now. You risk losing health, purpose, and focus.

The inflammation equation looks something like this:

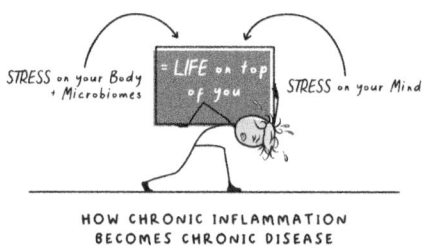

INFLAMMATION EQUATION

STRESS on your Body + Microbiomes = LIFE on top of you STRESS on your Mind

HOW CHRONIC INFLAMMATION
BECOMES CHRONIC DISEASE

Inflammation is diagnosable as a "disease" with a fancy (and misleading) name only when an organ or system dysregulates into dysfunction. Organs affected may include the heart, lungs, kidneys, stomach, colon, liver, nerves, or glands (thyroid, pineal, prostate, adrenals, pancreas, etc). Systems may be muscular-skeletal, immune, cardiovascular, digestive, nervous, endocrine, etc.

DISEASES OF CHRONIC INFLAMMATION

Scan your personal and family history for:

- Allergies and asthma
- All autoimmune diseases
- Cardiovascular diseases
- Joint diseases, including arthritis
- Organ diseases
- Cancer
- Obesity and diabetes
- Lung and respiratory diseases
- Alzheimer's, dementia

Remember, symptoms of inflammation are warning flares that your habits are conventional. See the symptoms as just that—a signal to change something *now*. Jump ahead to PRIMAL HABITS if you're ready to experiment.

Epidemic levels of chronic inflammation only picked up speed about 50 years ago. Chronic symptoms are a modern phenomenon. In 1935, 7.5% of American adults had a chronic disease. Today we're at 60%+ with a solid trajectory towards even more suffering. Over 85% of healthcare costs go on treating chronic inflammation—not prevention or resolution.[1]

CHRONIC DISEASE PREVALENCE IN AMERICA

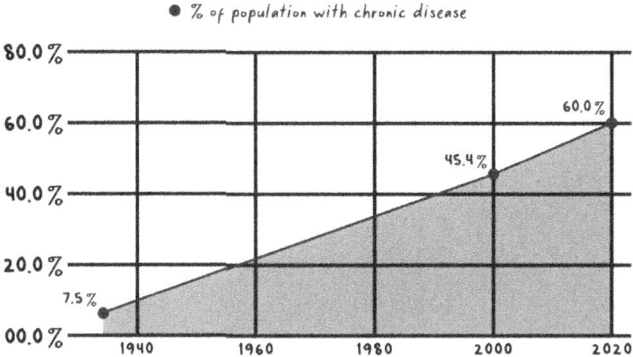

● % of population with chronic disease

Primary causes are daily diet and lifestyle habits. Degenerative changes are the result, due to intake of sugar, vegetable oils, engineered foods, and the herbicide glyphosate, which shows up in almost all conventional foods.[2]

Today, three out of five people suffer the consequences of chronic inflammation for years or decades, before dying a long, slow death. Accelerated aging is now starting in utero and during childhood. All the major lethal diseases for humans on the planet right now have their roots in chronic systemic inflammation:[3]

CHRONIC INFLAMMATORY DISEASES

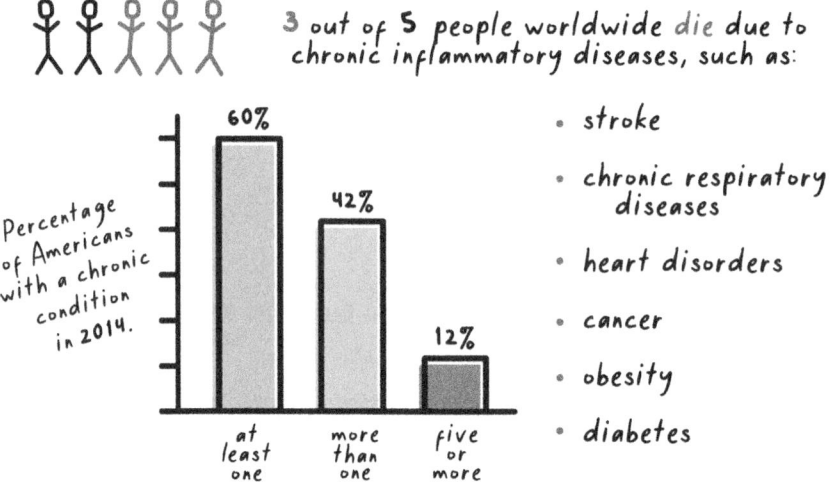

3 out of 5 people worldwide die due to chronic inflammatory diseases, such as:

- stroke
- chronic respiratory diseases
- heart disorders
- cancer
- obesity
- diabetes

Even fetuses pick up inflammatory markers. Nearly 30% of our children are on drugs for chronic diseases caused by conventional habits. We've stolen our children's health. The World Health Organization's global projections anticipate persistent increases through 2050-2060. Imagine that—not experiencing a functional body while growing up.[4]

Conventional habits have done nothing for our looks, our desires, our sex drive, or ability to reproduce. We've traded being the wisest of the wise mammals, engineered by nature to bring forth cultures of joy and connection, for the bloat of "too much." Too much to do, too much food, too much stimulation, too much stuff, too many pesticides, too much... too much. The poor, the under-resourced and underprivileged, those with lower IQ, those least equipped to succeed, suffer the most and the longest. We're rushed out of our time-honored rhythms, and now here we stand; in debt, without security, without integrity.[5]

I'll show two trajectories: A to B for better health; A to C for chronic inflammation. Remember: "B" for "better", "C" for "chronic."

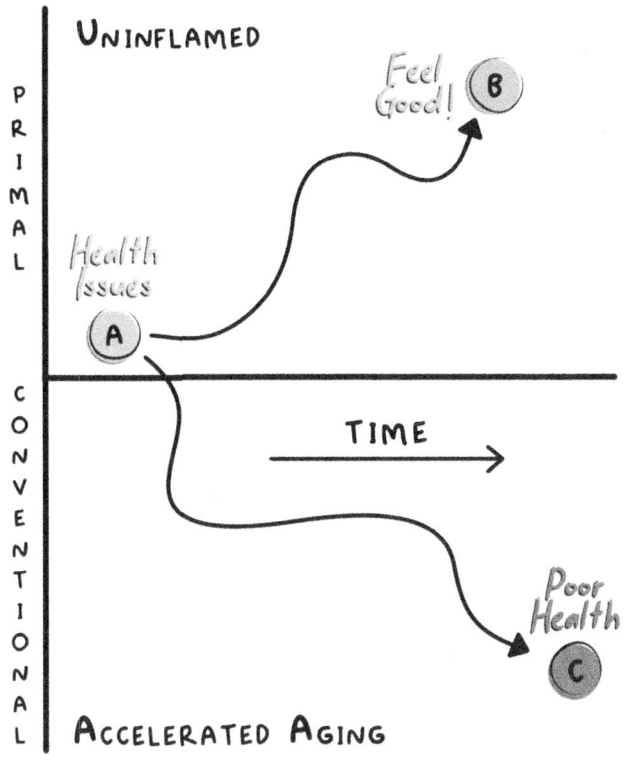

1. J. Nobbs. "What's Driving Chronic.Disease?" Jeffnobbs.com. 1 Jan. 2020, www.jeffnobbs.com/posts/whatcauses-chronic-disease.

2. C. Gillam. (2021, September 27). *Glyphosate Fact Sheet: Cancer and Other Health Concerns.* U.S. Right to Know. Retrieved June 18, 2022, from https://usrtk.org/pesticides/glyphosate-health-concerns/

3. Andrée-Anne Houde, et al. "Fetal Epigenetic Programming of Adipokines." Adipocyte, vol. 2, no. 1, 2013, pp. 41–46. doi:10.4161/adip.22055.; Furman, David, et al. "Chronic Inflammation in the Etiology of Disease Across the Life Span." Nature Medicine, vol. 25, no. 12, 2019, pp. 1822–32. doi:10.1038/s41591-019-0675-0.

4. Roma Pahwa, et al. "Chronic Inflammation." StatPearls [Internet], StatPearls Publishing, 2021, www.ncbi.nlm.nih.gov/books/NBK493173/#.

5. Tierney K. Lorenz. "Interactions Between Inflammation and Female Sexual Desire and Arousal Function." Current Sexual Health Reports, vol. 11, no. 4, 2019, pp. 287–99. doi:10.1007/s11930-019-00218-7.

Solutions

You never find yourself until you face the truth.

Pearl Bailey: *The Raw Pearl*

Our ancestors didn't suffer from chronic inflammation. They passed their genome forward, enduring weather exposure, viruses, bacteria, and food scarcity; and eventually all they had become, became... us. Their brains were 10% larger than ours. Chronic inflammation is dehumanizing us as a species.[1]

Conventional habits wear you down each day, decaying what makes you... you. In the cult of too-frequent calories, we've dulled our senses, polluted our cells, and fogged the inner navigation which orients life towards purpose. Chronic inflammation lowers cognitive function, diminishing our ability to think and learn, to be fired up about our collective future. Not to mention that the inflammatory bloat doesn't feel good or build confidence from the inside out.

Chronic inflammation begets chronic *allo*stasis, the opposite state of health that is *homeo*stasis. Allostasis literally means you aren't standing in yourself, you're filled with "other." Homeostasis means you are standing in yourself, and your body is healthy. I'll explain this in the section CHRONIC.

With chronic allostasis, the body is in a state of disease. *Allo*pathic medicine addresses disease, not health. Doctors are trained—even coerced—to treat diseases with drugs, rather than to cure chronic states at the behavioral or habit level, which would prevent people from becoming patients in the first place.

As science progresses, understandings and even definitions change. Today, we've mapped much of the human microbiome, yet the human virome, which feeds the microbiome, is a black hole (see MICROBIOME chapter). We now know urine isn't sterile: it's probiotic and prebiotic. We know that a pro-inflammatory environment, anywhere from your digestive tract to your bloodstream, disrupts DNA, causing cells to mutate. New scientific research has redefined the function of fat tissue as an endocrine organ designed to balance blood sugar and the immune system. Yet, these scientific breakthroughs haven't changed how doctors work with patients.

Scientists and doctors need to know about the most relevant research on habits that reverse chronic inflammation. This book contains hundreds of pertinent citations related to the inflammation epidemic. They should also be aware of the research that is most needed next; research that could make the most significant dent in curing this epidemic.

The innovative wellness sector is increasingly aware of out-of-pocket spending, as people aren't getting their needs met by modern healthcare. From coaching and consulting to supplements; from apps and wearable apps to at-home testing, those working in wellness want to know where the market is heading and how to be relevant. This book is also a guide to that.

Regardless of your background, you have a vested interest in your one and only body.

You know the difference between positive and negative stress, even if you're unaware of it. Positive stress, known as "eustress," is often hard to do in the moment, but it makes you feel good and grow in the long run. Exercise, breathing exercises, fasting, cold showers, orienting towards long-term goals, and pressuring yourself into smart sleep habits, are all "eustressors." Positive stressors make you stronger and sharper by engaging in adversity, or doing the hard thing, and are also known as adversity habits.

Negative stress comes from activities that are easy to do in the moment, but which negatively affect you in the long run. Negative stressors make you weaker and duller and have a degenerative effect. Think overeating, sitting all day, staying up late, sleeping in, drinking or smoking. Negative stress = distress.

Chronic inflammation indicates that habits are negative stressors or degenerative (not regenerative) adversity habits. To beat inflammation, you need to prioritize eustress habits over distress habits. How can you tell which is which? I believe that, with a little practice and tuning in —*you will know*, without thinking about it. Read on, try a habit, and you'll be on your way.

POSITIVE STRESSORS

Positive stressors make you look like this:

BEFORE   **AFTER**

When you do hard things first, the rest of your life gets easier, and you get smarter. Primal habits ritualize eustress into daily habits that are essential for your long game, and align you to "rhythm" in your short game. Refined, you're more aware that rhythm organizes time.

Timing, indeed, is everything. The circadian rhythm is the body's internal clock that evolved our physiological processes, like the sleep-wake cycle, to coordinate mental and physical systems. Circadian is Latin for "around a day," and this human chronological rhythm is largely regulated by sunlight. Primal habits activate circadian rhythm, organize *you* in time, and relax you into focus. This reverses disease and turns back the clock on aging, opening the door to ease in longevity.

POSITIVE STRESSORS

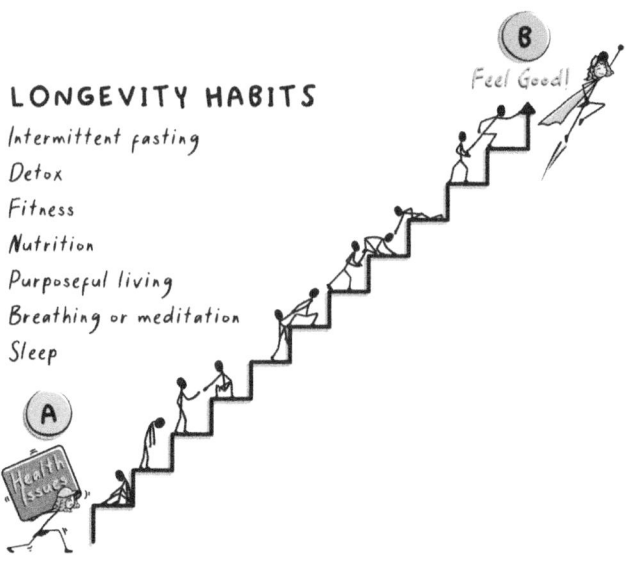

LONGEVITY HABITS

Intermittent fasting

Detox

Fitness

Nutrition

Purposeful living

Breathing or meditation

Sleep

Eastern religions and indigenous healing systems were inherently focused on eustress body/mind practices, as opposed to the model of sitting indoors in classrooms and lecture theaters found in modern schooling—the cognitive testing model. Eustressors develop your nerves, lungs, and mind and improve neuroplasticity and cognitive function. A resilient immune system relies on a robust nervous system and focused mind.

NEGATIVE STRESSORS

Widespread negative stressors include: chronic emotional stress; eating too much, too frequently, or too late; choosing short-term pleasure over long-term purpose; sacrificing sleep; and too much time sitting indoors. All cause chronic inflammation, oxidative stress, and distress (see CHRONIC).

NEGATIVE STRESSORS

Health Issues
(A)

Degenerative Habits
- snacking or eating late
- sedentary lifestyle
- convenience food
- short term decisions
- worry, negative thinking
- sacrificing sleep

Poor Health
(C)

Distress destroys the subtle biochemistry of the human being. Aging isn't designed to be painful or riddled with chronic disease. Negative stressors may be culturally prevalent, but they don't need to be, and haven't always been there. They degenerate your physiology, making it impossible to thrive.[2]

Conventional habits are the negative stressors that accelerate aging.

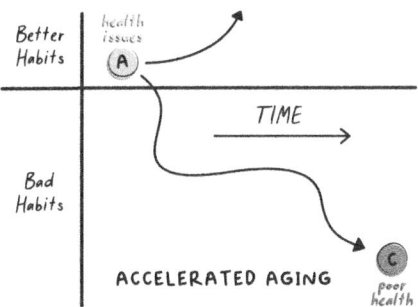

Better Habits

health issues
(A)

TIME

Bad Habits

ACCELERATED AGING

(C) poor health

SWITCH

The first teaching from the ancient Hindu healing system of Ayurveda is that, with intelligence and instincts earned and handed down over millennia, you can distinguish what is working for you from what isn't.

Good or bad, ease or disease, a vibrant long life depends on distinguishing good from bad for you.[3]

Charaka Samhita

The power is yours, the teaching implies. Think for yourself. Notice. Reflect. Adjust your behaviors.

Positive stressors organize you—from molecules to microbiome, from cells to community. Being with others who choose positive stressors is critical (see COMMUNE, FORGIVE, GROOVE, COOK).

Primal habits, like self-massage (RUB), are positive stressors that change your emotional state by releasing positive hormones like oxytocin. PEE upcycles relaxation hormones, and decreases stress hormones like cortisol. TRIP, PEE, COLD, SILENCE, and EXHALE are positive stressors that shift consciousness and uplevel your thinking and emotional state, for physiological anti-oxidizing, anti-inflammatory, anti-aging, and peak performance results.

Which habits you choose, and your next normal, determines how you feel each day and how much you reverse aging.[4]

1. Mark P. Mattson "An Evolutionary Perspective on Why Food Overconsumption Impairs Cognition." *Trends in cognitive sciences* vol. 23,3 (2019): 200-212. doi:10.1016/j.tics.2019.01.003
2. Bruce S. McEwen. "Stressed or Stressed Out: What Is the Difference?" Journal of Psychiatry and Neuroscience, vol. 30, no. 5, 2005, pp. 315–18.
3. *Hita hitam sukham dukham ayus tasya hitahitam.*
    P. K. Sharma and Charak Samhita Bhagwan Das (English translation). 6th ed., Chaukhamba Sanskrit series, Varanasi 221001, 2003.
4. T. Fulop, et al. "Immunology of Aging: The Birth of Inflammaging." Clinical Reviews in Allergy & Immunology, 2021, pp. 1–14. doi:10.1007/s12016-021-08899-6.

Primal Habits are Free

POTENTIAL TO THRIVE

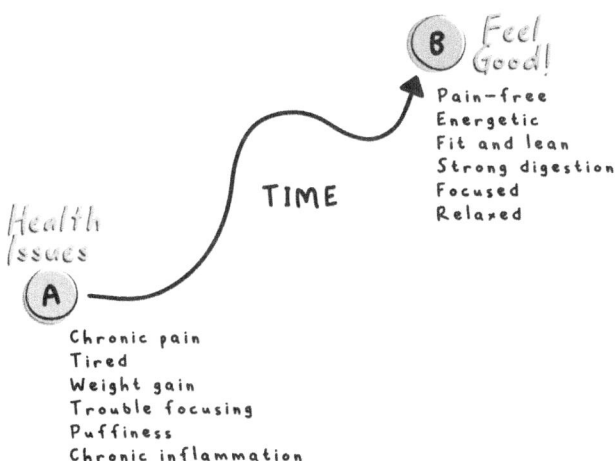

You eat less frequently and less food, you generate time, you find focus and ease. You eat smarter. You avoid the costs of illness (MEDICINE). As your body detoxes the bloat, the fog, the inflammation, you bestir your next purpose, aligned to meaning (see PURPOSE, FOCUS). You invest smarter because you get smarter. Addictive habits and degenerative behaviors fall away (see WISDOM).

What wakes up within you?

- Your body: your gut, your microbiome, spine, lungs, brain
- Your posture, your stride, your mobility
- Your senses
- Your mind
- Your core relationships
- Your goals
- Your potential

By necessity, our ancestors had the primal habits that reinvigorate homeostasis. Primal habits are both ancient *and* futuristic. Primal habits recover direction and smarten our cells through challenging, uncomfortable, positive stressors. Today, these anti-inflammatory stressors that make you resilient and adaptable need to be self-imposed.

Rewiring your habits from conventional to primal rewires your brain and nervous system into relaxed regeneration. As your habits become primal, your brain rewires to learn faster, which is termed neural plasticity, or neuroplasticity. You become more intelligent, more vital, more alive. Neurodegeneration reverses as you generate new neurons, positive emotions, new thoughts, and better opportunities (see FOCUS).

Rewilding is rewiring.

Primal habits turn on the cellular processes of "autophagy" and "apoptosis." Autophagy is the natural process of a cell removing dysfunctional or unnecessary components, and is activated by fasting. Apoptosis is intentional cell death due to it being damaged. These biological clean-up processes are what *uninflames* you at the cellular and intra-cellular level, waking up your genetic code and optimizing the environment around your genes, called your "epigenome." This extends the prime of your life, also known as your healthspan. You supersede the diseases of modern culture and the diseases of your ancestors by feeding your microbiome, which optimizes your DNA (see AUTOPHAGY, MICROBIOME, EPIGENETICS, FASTING).

So ask yourself, if a person is unhealthy, is it more important to know their *habits* or their *disease*?

PRIMAL HABITS

Chronic

The World Health Organization ranks disease caused by chronic inflammation as the greatest threat to human health. Yet, the promise of an instant fix with a magic pill is not helpful when inflammation has gone chronic. In this chapter, we'll look at what inflammation is, how it goes chronic, and the solutions.

Inflammation is defense. The immune system is called in to identify what is foreign or harmful, and take appropriate action to learn or heal. The immune system is forever adaptive and grows in knowing the matter evolving outside the body, in the forms of bacteria, viruses, etc.

Primal habits improve responsiveness to acute inflammation, assimilating new microbial species, and healing injuries.

Allo means "other," "different" or "opposing."

Stasis means "to stand."

Acute allostasis is the response to "other."

The adaptive immune system, in the acute state, cleans house by building antibodies to eat pathogenic viruses and bacteria. This cycle reestablishes homeostasis.

In the acute response, the pathogen attracts the immune system. Antibodies search and destroy pathogens by detecting the antigens on the surface of the pathogen.

The acute response looks like this:

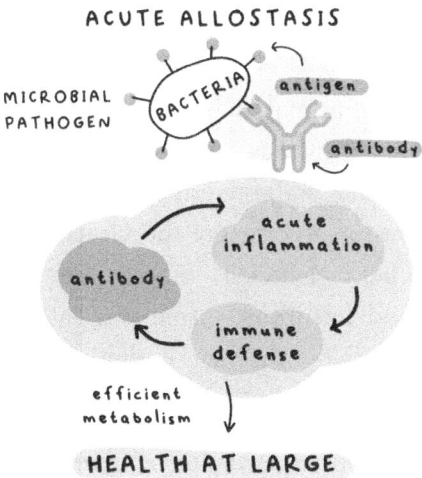

"Acute" and "chronic" are not the same. The same molecules that are necessary for an acute immune response—one that leads to a positive outcome in a healthy system—actually become the generators and inducers of inflammation in an unhealthy internal environment.

Systems go haywire in a polluted internal environment, generated by conventional reality.

Our immune system acts as a "double-edged sword" that can either heal or harm that is based on differentiating between the "self"' and the "non-self"' and destroying only those tissues that are recognized as "non-self." [1]

Chao Liu: *Cytokines: From Clinical Significance to Quantification*

Homeo means "alike, similar." Think of it as cells of the same body existing harmoniously.

Homeostasis is essential for healthspan. Healthspan is the part of a person's life in which they are in good health.

Humans evolved with primal habits that kept a tight ship at the molecular level. The farm was a complete ecosystem. Crops were fertilized by urine and composted feces from mammals, including humans. All food was organic before the Green Revolution following World War II. Synthetic chemicals left over from the war found new uses as pesticides and fertilizers, introducing a new hardship on an immune system that didn't evolve in a synthetic toxin environment.

The other major toxin is overeating. The body can't digest all of the inputs it receives, so particles at the molecular level create junk in the system. These undigested particles are the major toxins that ruin the body atmosphere at every level, molecular, cellular, and holistic (See ALLOSTASIS).

WHY UNDIGESTED FOOD?

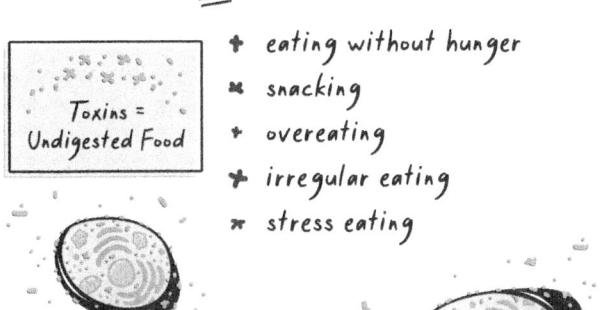

Toxins = Undigested Food

✦ eating without hunger

✖ snacking

✦ overeating

✦ irregular eating

✶ stress eating

Unhealthy Cells

These toxins are identified by the immune system as "foreign matter." Fair enough. But, when the internal atmosphere, the environment around and within your cells, becomes toxic, then you've got trouble. The body has lost its integrity, its ability to recognize itself.

When this happens, cells are swimming in chemical confusion, navigating the chronic crisis of a polluted environment... and this begets a state of disease. Your allostatic load reflects the state of disease present, or "standing," within you.

ALLOSTATIC LOAD

In chronic inflammation, allostasis is constantly in effect. Homeostasis, the natural, harmonious state of self-recognition, drifts out of reach.

That which induces the ongoing production of inflammation is termed a "chronic inducer." Inducers are the range of toxins listed above—from synthetic chemicals to overeating. Many inducers are *anthropogens* - meaning produced by the body, as opposed to *pathogens*, which are bacteria and viruses. Either way, immune cells are recruited to clean up "otherness."

Because habits are habits, inducers generate ongoing stimulus. Immune cells now chronically generate inflammation to mediate the "otherness." Inducers are further generated by cells under distress, as part of the inflammation cycle gone into a chronic state.

This becomes a feedback loop, or chronic pathway, that looks like this:

→ inflammation inducers → immune cells recruited → immune cells secrete inflammatory mediators → tissue degenerates, becomes an inflammatory inducer →

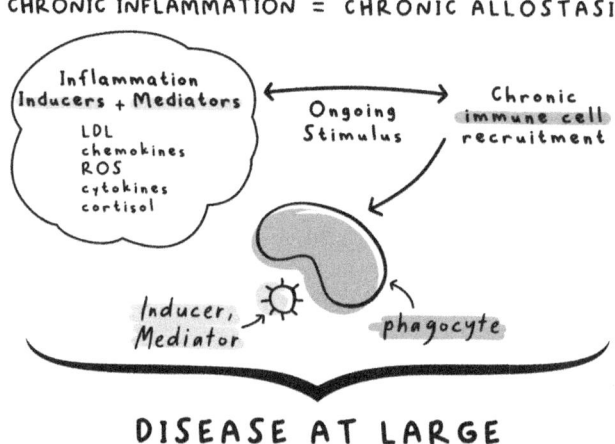

CHRONIC INFLAMMATION = CHRONIC ALLOSTASIS

DISEASE AT LARGE

Resources from the immune system keep going into clean-up rather than optimization of health. You're stuck. You're chronic.

This chronic inflammation cycle destroys the microbiome, which human DNA cells rely on for cell replication. Cells can't function properly, let alone replicate without degeneration or mutation (see chapters: MICROBIOME, EPIGENETICS, NITRIC OXIDE).

The feedback loop causes tissue damage. In allopathic medicine, our sick-care model, disease becomes diagnosable when tissue is no longer functional. Chronic inflammation diseases are diagnosed in association with another medical condition.[2] There are currently no highly effective laboratory measures to assess patients exclusively for chronic inflammation. Yet, the symptoms shown in the list CHECK YOUR SYMPTOMS (at the beginning of this book) are all precursors to chronic disease, caused by the habits that generate chronic inflammation.

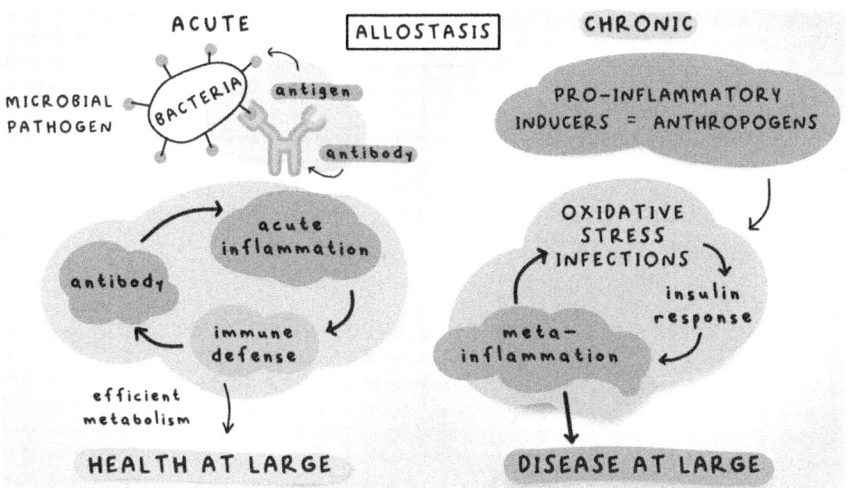

Other types of cells grow as dumping grounds for "other," such as tumors or polyps, fibrosis or lesions, some of which may be cancerous. All are detrimental and show a confused and dysfunctional internal atmosphere entering a level of internal disease gone into survival mode, which eventually leads to systems shutting down. No more healthspan.

(Note: it's important at this point to differentiate between "healthspan" and "lifespan." The first, as I mentioned, is the period of life spent in good health. The second is the entire span of an individual life. Prolonged lifespan with allostatic load is assisted by synthetic chemicals and surgeries, without addressing the underlying allostatic load and compromised healthspan. Allostatic load dysregulates the body, shortening first healthspan, then lifespan.)[3]

As you become increasingly toxic, the immune system doesn't have the resources to adapt to new pathogens, whether that's a supersized meal, a coronavirus, or a new chemical in your household cleaner. Immune resources aren't available for healing, repair, or advancement.

Remember, the immune system evolved with acute response to allostasis made possible by primal habits, especially from fasting, eating organic and local, and living without chemicals.

UNCHECKED

As the immune system breaks, diseased tissue spreads through organs and systems. Cancer, heart disease, autoimmune diseases (like rheumatoid arthritis), diabetes, asthma, cancer, infections, dementia; the list caused by the chronic crisis is growing.[4]

SYMPTOMS INDICATIVE OF DISEASE PROCESS

#ACCELERATEDAGING

(A)

Health Issues

Tired
Overweight
Bloated
Easily distracted
Brain fog
Chronic inflammation

(C)

Poor Health

Disease-at-large
Disease of any organ
e.g. Heart, liver, lung
Cancer
Immune disease
Autoimmune disease

TIME

The toxic waste of the chronic inflammation cycle disrupts the endocrine system. The endocrine system mediates systems-wide communication and regulates immune response. The immune system acting in a state of confusion can't recognize self, as in autoimmune disease. The line between self and pathogen gets blurry. Chronic "otherness" interferes with "self." You are not at home in yourself.

With chronic overeating, inflammation becomes meta-inflammation, which disrupts metabolic cells.[5]

When things are chronic, homeostasis is not possible. A chronic state of *other*—of not standing in yourself—has become the norm. The worse you feel, in yourself or about yourself, the higher your allostatic load, the higher your negative bias, the less able you are to motivate yourself to help yourself.

But—good news! Primal habits, and people who live them, get you re-established in the seat of yourself, in homeostasis, reversing the damage of chronic. Interestingly, with training in primal habits, allostatic load becomes a kind of awareness, giving you control over how much integrity you are willing to compromise in a given phase of life.

In Ayurvedic medicine, there are six stages of the disease process, from the accumulation of an imbalance, to aggravation, to disease spreading through organ systems. Chronic inflammation is detectable by symptoms in the first three stages of disease, when it's in the microbiomes, the digestive tract, and the bloodstream. Chronic disease shows up in the last three stages, as inflammation disrupts cells into dysfunction to the point of specific tissues and systems losing function.

OVEREATING = ACCELERATED AGING

If you don't feel at home in yourself, start doing the primal habits with us, and find holistic healers in your community who understand how to reverse the first few stages of chronic inflammation.

POWER TO CHANGE

What you acknowledge, you have the power to change.

Primal habits demolish the allostatic load, returning physiology to homeostasis. To be homeostatic is to be seated in the self, or what the yogis call *svastha,* synonymous with health. Your cells turn the tide from degenerating toward regenerating. You reverse accelerated aging by actively investing in your healthspan. Then, allostasis arises as a response to a pathogen, not as a daily experience.

At CLUB THRIVE, we've guided hundreds of people with chronic inflammation to reverse the damage that had been building for decades. We find that, with guidance and support, this takes about a year in our program, CLUB THRIVE. That's why it's a year-long membership, funnily enough!

---

1. Chao Liu, et al. "Cytokines: From Clinical Significance to Quantification." Advanced Science, vol. 8, no. 15, 2021, e2004433. doi:10.1002/advs.202004433.
2. R. Pahwa, A. Goyal, I. Jialal. Chronic Inflammation. [Updated 2021 Sep 28]. In: StatPearls [Internet]. Treasure Island (FL): StatPearls Publishing; 2022 Jan-. Available from: https://www.ncbi.nlm.nih.gov/books/NBK493173/
3. Yara J. Toenders, et al. "Inflammation and Depression in Young People: A Systematic Review and Proposed Inflammatory Pathways." Molecular Psychiatry, vol. 27, no. 1, 2022, pp. 315–27. doi:10.1038/s41380-021-01306-8.; Xie, Wanze, et al. "Chronic Inflammation Is Associated with Neural Responses to Faces in Bangladeshi Children." NeuroImage, vol. 202, 2019, p. 116110. doi:10.1016/j.neuroimage.2019.116110; Calcaterra, Valeria, et al. "Evaluation of Allostatic Load as a Marker of Chronic Stress in Children and the Importance of Excess Weight." Frontiers in Pediatrics, vol. 7, 2019, p. 335. doi:10.3389/fped.2019.00335.
4. Harvard Health. "Fighting Inflammation." 1 Jan. 2022, www.health.harvard.edu/staying-healthy/understanding-inflammation. Accessed 23 Apr. 2022.
5. Chuan Li, et al. "Macrophage Polarization and Meta-Inflammation." Translational Research, vol. 191, 2018, pp. 29–44. doi:10.1016/j.trsl.2017.10.004.

Medicine

> Wherever the art of medicine is loved, there is also a love of humanity.
>
> Hippocrates

What is the *best* medicine for chronic inflammation? What is *your* best medicine?

CAN DRUGS HEAL THE CHRONIC BODY?

Modern medicine, including medical education and technology, was founded on the principle of treating acute conditions, rather than preventing and curing the roots of chronic inflammation. Drugs are fabulous for acute conditions: pain killers, antibiotics, antivirals, anesthetics; for treating accidents, injuries, surgeries, acute infections.

But for chronic inflammation?

Chronic inflammation is habit-driven. It started slowly when we began farming 10,000 years ago, and scaled up quickly with revolution after revolution; from farm to factory to industrialized chemical farming. Each revolution changed how people worked and what we understood (and standardized) as "food."[1]

The habits that trigger chronic are those that have shifted from primal to conventional: in diet, too frequent and too many calories; a loss of microbes and enzymes in our food; not enough movement or sleep; chemicals our bodies can't process. The chronic stress of living against the circadian rhythm (a rhythm that sets body clocks into harmony) makes us feel like we're working against the clock, rather than supported by daily cycles in time.

Drugs for chronic inflammation can help a little with symptoms, but they can't heal the underlying habits generating chronic inflammation (see HEAL).

It's a deception of the first order.

Pharmaceuticals give hope that a resolution to chronic issues is possible without changing what we do, how we are, in our lives. They promise cure without change, without effort. Without impacting the root cause of chronic inflammation, they often make us feel temporarily better, but only by suppressing symptoms and, quite often, through the "placebo effect" (a placebo is used in a control group of an experiment to have no real effect and to test the treatment). Relief of symptoms in the short term via pharmaceuticals trends, almost inevitably, toward more prescriptions—more drugs—and these cause more and more side effects, which call for more and more drugs, which piles on even more allostatic load, and the end result is more chronic disease in the long term. Putting out fire with gasoline. It's a tragic and all-too-familiar story.[2]

This is why people on a drug end up on more than one drug, sooner or later, rather than becoming healthy.

UNREGULATED

Lex Fridman interviewed the author of *Overdosed America,* John Abramson (you can find it on YouTube). He is a family physician and public health policy professor at Harvard Medical School. The discussion highlights the problems big pharma is creating in society, including why doctors push allopathic drugs for chronic diseases rather than coach holistic lifestyle upgrades:

LEX FRIDMAN: There is an entire mechanism established for testing drugs. There isn't an entire mechanism established in terms of scientific rigor for testing lifestyle changes.

Money can buy ignorance, I suppose, in science.

JOHN ABRAMSON: Money can buy blinders that are on, that don't look outside the reductionist model. And that is another issue. Nobody says to doctors in training, 'Only listen to reductionist studies and conclusions and methods of promoting health.' Nobody says that explicitly. But the respectable science has to do with controlling the factors.

It just doesn't make sense to me to allow a drug to be advertised as preventing cardiovascular disease when you haven't included lifestyle changes as an arm in the study. It's just so crystal clear that the purpose of that study is to sell [the drug]; it's not to prevent cardiovascular disease. If we were in charge, I would try to convince you that anywhere the results of that study were presented to physicians, it would be stamped in big red letters: *"This study did not compare* [the drug] *to lifestyle changes."* The doctors are trained to kind of forget that that's not there.[3]

Later in the conversation, Abramson clarifies that the government institutions meant to protect public health, like the FDA, are currently mechanized to protect big pharma.

Doctors are trying to get through the day with too many patients in too little time. They aren't employed to keep up with the past decade of scientific research on microbiome, epigenetics, and lifestyle changes, nor is the medical system they work in financially or operationally structured to guide lifestyle change.

Drugs not used in concert with lifestyle changes essentially suppress symptoms and layer on side effects, which creates a need for more medication. We'll investigate those statistics later in MONEY.

The frustration with pharmaceutical medicine is that it's *allopathic*: driven to medicate disease, rather than *holistic*: driven towards optimization and lifelong healthspan, or extending the prime of your life. The difference in orientations leads to outcomes miles apart on the health spectrum. Drugs are not tested for efficacy against diet and lifestyle-habit upgrades.

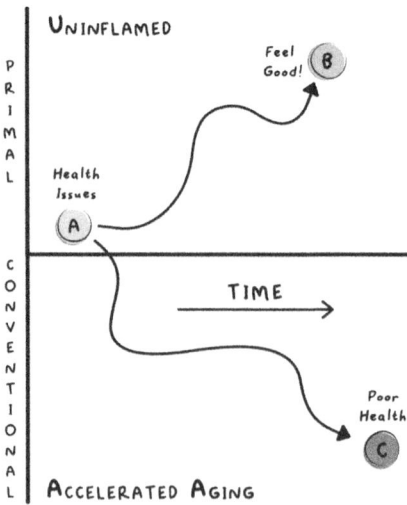

Drugs—from antibiotics to anti-depressants (SSRIs), from opioids to anti-inflammatories (NSAIDS)—wreak havoc on the microbiome. Drugs cause "dysbiosis"—when a part of the microbial ecosystem is controlled by pathogenic bacteria, it has become "dysbiotic." Dysbiosis becomes a pro-inflammatory feedback loop, hindering digestion, dulling emotional sensitivity, and having countless indirect side effects (see MICROBIOME).[4]

When you only use drugs for chronic inflammation (without habit coaching) you delay the "volatility" already in the system. By delaying volatility, you layer on even more allostatic load (see CHRONIC). Like suppressing forest fires, you set the stage for catastrophic destruction later. Like the desperate act of printing money to stabilize a weakened economy, with drugs you paper over the cracks, you attempt to resolve errors without taking any substantive action; and only such action would create a responsive market that could correct itself (see MONEY).

If your preference is to avoid change now, all you do is store up more suffering for your future. The debt grows and grows. And when that debt gets called in, will you be ready to pay the price?

So, how overdosed are modern humans?

PHARMADEMIC

Canada spends half its taxpayer dollars on conventional treatments for the chronic body, not on uprooting chronic. Unfortunately, the investment yields an opposite outcome. As citizens, we've become consumers of "sick-care," not healthcare.[5]

70% of Americans take at least one prescription medication. More than 50% take at least two. According to the Mayo Clinic, the most common prescriptions are: antibiotics, antihypertensives, antidepressants, and opioid painkillers. The US population, by age, using one or more prescription drugs is around 30% (adolescents); 50% (adults); and 85%

(elders). Humans, as a species, are drugged by these pharmaceutical synthetic chemicals at epidemic rates in a mass experiment unprecedented in human history.[6]

Elders are the easiest target for drug companies. In developed countries, taxpayer dollars generally cover drugs for the elderly, and elders vote to ensure this continues. Aging with chronic inflammation symptoms and diseases is horrible—but the suffering can't be solved with pills.

Resolution of the conflict between environment and our ancient genome might be the only effective manner for "healthy aging," and to achieve this we might have to return to the lifestyle of the Paleolithic era as translated to the 21st century culture.[7]

Ruiz-Núñez: *Lifestyle and Nutritional Imbalances Associated with Western Diseases*

Thinking a wonder drug will be your solution for chronic inflammation, without doing the work of Paleolithic habits, screws up your relationship with reality. You miss the wake-up calls that are trying to alert you to your current fragility. You afflict your future self.

For this book, and the approach I'm advocating, I've named these Paleolithic lifestyle habits "primal." Like prime numbers, they are irreducible. "Primal" encompasses our original habits, our evolutionary nature; primary and radical.

The food industry, advertising industry, big pharma, and healthcare (tied to the financial services sector and big media) make short-term gains for stockholders at the expense of species-wide chronic inflammation. Shareholders and stockholders are trapped, too, in a system generating profit while we degenerate—while we *all* degenerate. No one's family is immune to the effects of the chronic pandemic.

Oh, for the love of humanity!

Hippocrates would not impressed.

The lack of integrity and big-picture solutions from the industries that manipulate culture means that citizens need to become more self-reliant and responsible for their own self-care.

But not all drugs are bad—and this is where you see that my perspective is futurist as well as ancient-traditionalist. The exciting engineering of new targeted drugs, like DNA methylation inhibitors and next-generation microbiome modulators, are tailored to re-engineer the microbiome and epigenome. If paired with lifestyle habits that turn the tide of a pro-inflammatory environment to a regenerative one, we could see sustainable, predictable health miracles happen in real-time. The call to action for big pharma is to test drugs with, and against, lifestyle changes.

But, back to you, as a citizen, as you become self-reliant in the fight to beat inflammation. Start with a Ulysses contract.

MAKE A ULYSSES CONTRACT

Symptoms of chronic inflammation are meant to force our hand. To wake up. To develop anti-fragile habits of resilience.

Your symptoms should make you ask yourself:

1. *How good do I want to feel?*
2. *Which habits are working for me right now?*
3. *Which habits aren't working for me?*

A "Ulysses contract" is what you make to bind yourself to your own better future; named after the Greek hero Ulysses, who tied himself to his ship's mast when passing the bewitching sirens. The sirens lured sailors with their song onto the rocks of their island, leading them to shipwreck and destruction—which here is the disaster of habit and hedonism, devoid of meaning. Ulysses the hero committed to doing the hard thing now for a better future later.

Make a contract with yourself, *right now*.

How good do you want to feel? Commit to that vision. Notice your mindset shift towards the positive, the possible. What do you want more than the allure of contemporary convenience and numbing comfort?

Or, if Ulysses doesn't fire your imagination, think of it as a "deathbed perspective"—what would you regret, lying on your deathbed? The snacks, the booze, the Netflix and chill, were they all worth the slow decline into illness, drugs, disability and pain? That really pulls your potential into the now.

Do you want, instead, to look back from your deathbed and say *I gave it my best shot?* Do you want to look back and say to yourself, *I was humble enough to learn what experience taught me? My breakdowns led to breakthroughs.*

You can think of the breakthrough/breakdown cycle—the natural growth/compost cycle—as one that orients towards depth (compost) in order to gain the energy, the momentum for growth. If you approach the stage of breakdown as one of opportunity (what falls apart has the chance to come back together in a new way) you will begin to see that you are not stuck in a cycle of suffering—you are making progress. You're not stuck on a wheel; you're moving up in an evolutionary spiral, travelling toward higher-order living as you go around. It may be painful, but you're getting somewhere. Your future is one of greater self-actualization and integration. Roots in the earth, the underworld of hell suffering; shoots and fruits to heaven. Like all things that grow, you need those roots to power you upwards.

YOUR MINDSET = YOUR FUTURE

BREAKTHROUGH

Obstacles
+
Challenges

Next-Level
Competences

EGO
Ahamkara

BREAKDOWN

Your FUTURE
should be BIGGER + BRIGHTER
than your PAST.

Looking back...

Deathbed
Perspective

Dan Sullivan

50 55 60 65 70

i am here now   six feet under

Rewiring habits is the way out of the pain cave. Our strategy, to reverse all things chronic and engage your edge, is to use positive stressor habits that reactivate circadian rhythm and nourish the microbiome's terrain (see SCIENCE ADDENDUM).

Preference your future self over your conventional habits.

SELF-STUDY AS MEDICINE: N=1

You are designed to uphold a highly organized environment within your cells as you age through the decades. You are designed to be relaxed and self-directed. Inflammatory activations are for acute crises only.

The yogis prioritized self-study as essential to optimizing the self (see SANSKRIT GLOSSARY, *svadyaya*). With self-study, you double down on what is working and delete what isn't. You swing the pendulum to get pulsation (see HUNGER, CHANNELS).

The longstanding truth from ancient medicine is self-study: learn from yesterday to smarten up today. You ditch all habits that generate inflammation.

Even for the biohackers, primal habits may challenge their beliefs.

Test the habits. Verify for yourself. "N=1" is your personal data set, your experiment and experience. It's singular, uniquely yours, and it's where you'll learn the most. The yogis would add that it's gravely important to you because it's how you navigate your next experiment with reality. Your personal data will lead to more improvement than any other.

For a primal human, medicine is everywhere. The primal habits re-engage your senses, your true hunger, your ability to steer towards profundity.

PERSONALIZED

There is an opportunity, now, for a more specialized fit for you, with the habits waiting to be found through personalized medicine. This can be done with "body typing," which was common in indigenous wisdom; it's a way to personalize healthcare (see BODY TYPE).

Your body type is evident in your metabolic tendencies, physical characteristics, and mental and emotional proclivities. Your innate strengths and weaknesses show up as a pattern, a constitution.

In the BODY TYPE section, you will find out how you can tailor your habits so that they are specific to you and your well-being. Better to steer the ship with the correct manual, right?

To thrive, you must organize yourself.

Primal habits organize you internally, within yourself, your cells, your microbiome, and your virome. Your nature co-evolved with Nature. Primal habits also organize you externally, with your people and place, by aligning your rhythm.

When you zoom out your perspective, you see we're one human species on one special planet. The one-size-fits-all approach to conquering chronic is: primal habits.

Ditch the conventional habits. Which *un*conventional habits are your best medicine? Let's find out.

---

1. Begoña Ruiz-Núñez, et al. "Lifestyle and Nutritional Imbalances Associated with Western Diseases: Causes and Consequences of Chronic Systemic Low-Grade Inflammation in an Evolutionary Context." *The Journal of Nutritional Biochemistry,*

vol. 24, no. 7, 2013, pp. 1183–201. *Crossref*, https://doi.org/10.1016/j.jnutbio.2013.02.009.

2. Arthur Zuckerman. "46 Placebo Effect Statistics: 2020/2021 Data, Examples & Implications." CompareCamp. 27 May 2020, comparecamp.com/placebo-effect-statistics/. Accessed 23 Apr. 2022.

3. Lex Fridman. "John Abramson: Big Pharma | Lex Fridman Podcast #263." YouTube. 11 Feb. 2022, www.youtube.com/watch?v=arrokG3wCdE.; minutes 28-33 (section: Advertising).

4. Peter Sjöstedt, et al. "Serotonin Reuptake Inhibitors and the Gut Microbiome: Significance of the Gut Microbiome in Relation to Mechanism of Action, Treatment Response, Side Effects, and Tachyphylaxis." Frontiers in Psychiatry, vol. 12, 2021, p. 682868. doi:10.3389/fpsyt.2021.682868; Bosco, Nabil, and Mario Noti. "The Aging Gut Microbiome and Its Impact on Host Immunity." Genes and Immunity, vol. 22, 5-6, 2021, pp. 289–303. doi:10.1038/s41435-021-00126-8.

5. "Infections, Inflammation and Chronic Diseases in the Changing Environment." *Research.Ucalgary.Ca*, University of Calgary, Canada, Nov. 2015, research.ucalgary.ca/sites/default/files/IICD/iicd-research-strategy-2015.pdf.

6. "Cures and Curses: A History of Pharmaceutical Advertising in America." University of St. Augustine for Health Sciences Library. 1 Jan. 2022, library.usa.edu/Cures-Curses-Exhibit. Accessed 23 Apr. 2022.

7. Ruiz-Núñez, et al. "Lifestyle and Nutritional Imbalances Associated with Western Diseases",1183–201.

Wisdom

On the path to smarter habits you churn your experiences into wisdom. You discover truth. The wiser you become, the more you trust yourself, and the better you design your experience. You own what you know and who you've become. Thus, wisdom is your best long-haul investment.

The surest path to wisdom is with the help of a growth community, which usually includes a strong guide. In a growth community, you can make friends with people who have smarter habits and more wisdom in the arenas you, yourself, want growth or depth.

The true potential of money, after mere subsistence, is the benefit it can bring you beyond the mundane and the material. It has the potential to push you forward into deeper fulfillment, well-being, awareness, and a meaningful legacy, if you learn to use it wisely.

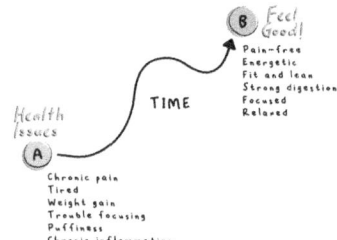

POTENTIAL TO THRIVE

To use your money well, it's helpful to articulate what you value both in the now and in the future you want to see for yourself. Articulate what is worthy of your investment. Think, and then speak, about what has true value: that's where your money should go next. Remember, you thriving is always your own best investment (see WISDOM).

Ask yourself, what will gain value rather than lose value with time?

GROWTH COMMUNITIES

Our nerves are networked (see COMMUNE). Networks are better because humans are an ultra-social species.

The need for the experience of community has only intensified. Even with all the ways to connect, we live and function in ways that keep us isolated. Without new ways to come together, this isolation will persist.[1]

Peter Block: *Community: The Structure of Belonging*

We evolve more completely when we do it together. Words from many cultures point to coming together in growth groups: *kula, sangha, posse, team, tribe, troupe, band, club*. Groups have a *leader, captain, guide, chief, guru,* or *coach* (see LEAD).

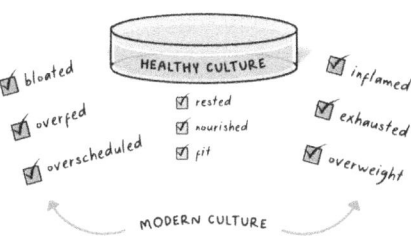

Block asks: "where can your good will make a real difference?" Peter Block is an expert on community, he says the shift from consumer to citizen begins with paying attention to your inner "give-a-shitter."

Ask yourself. What could you actually do with your good will? That is where *you* belong next. When you know what you'll do with your good will, you start to belong somewhere, to something. Then, Peter explains, "belong" has a second meaning:

The second meaning of the word **belong** has to do with being an owner: Something belongs to me. To belong to a community is to act as a creator and co-owner of that community. What I consider mine I will build and nurture.

So, to belong, you commit to being part of where you can make a tangible difference, and you take ownership of your actions and your collective's actions. Block continues:

The communal possibility rotates on the question, "What can we create together?" This emerges from the social space we create when we're together. It's shaped by the nature of the culture within which we operate but isn't controlled by it. This question of what we can create together is at the intersection of possibility and accountability.[2]

Possibility of designing the future together; accountability for what happens.

You'll want teammates and accountability partners to ensure you improve your game. You'll want guidance from experts, until you become an expert. By then, you'll be friends with the guides. You'll be embedded, innovating within the collaborative culture.

Strong growth communities have:

1. A shared vision, a way to communicate.
2. Infrastructure for members to develop, step-by-step, towards their desired end result.
3. A guide or guides who have already walked the path to the desired end result and are committed to guiding the members to their desired outcomes.
4. An investment requirement, known as members having"skin in the game." This creates member commitment that leads to potency for both the group and each member.
5. Periodic open-door events, like social mixers, for those on the outside to see what's happening on the inside.

A growth community may be a coaching or mastermind group, an interactive training program, or a mission-driven business or non-profit organization.

Look for a group that embodies the values you're looking for, and looks likely to help you toward your desired next experiences. Find a community that is thriving and whose members are clearly thriving. Get to know the guide. Investigate until you verify you want to get on the inside track. Questioning is good. Scratch, sniff, look online, ask around, and don't take any one person's or source's word. The Buddha, in a famous sutra, stated the wisdom of taking nothing on trust. Test everything against your own first-hand experience. A guide or leader who doesn't allow themselves to be questioned is almost certainly not the real deal.

GUIDED TRANSFORMATION

The economic value ladder is an analysis developed by economics, describing what humans value as economies develop. As hunter-gatherers in our instinctual mammalian survival, we coexisted with nature without economic exchange. As we developed agriculture about 10,000 years ago, we grew crops as a commodity that could be stored or traded. As storage crops developed, people stopped migrating and began to urbanize. People made goods and traded goods. People offered services and traded those for goods and commodities. Now, goods and services have become so available (in affluent societies) that many are turning toward experiences—think a trip to Disneyland or Burning Man festival, or watching Netflix, or going to a World Cup match.

As humans are wired for growth, experiences become customized for transformation—a new development of economic activity in which experiences are not just provided in a one-size-fits-all form, but are designed and intended to be profound, unique, life-changing; "transformative." According to economists, we value guided transformation, individualized or differentiated for our particular wants —and we are willing to pay a premium for it. Of course, if you don't have enough goods and services (aka food, shelter, clothes, laundry) you won't be investing in guided transformation; unless you are of a monastic bent. When one's material possession bucket is full, you ponder meaning. Then, the desire for depth, for transformation, arises. Think back to the most transformational experiences of your life, how they arose, and if there were structures to guide the transformation.

The economic underpinnings of our society are advancing toward transformative experiences that are qualitative and beneficial to body, mind and spirit. You can see this in the economic value ladder, where guided transformation is exchanged for money at premium value and premium pricing. Humans value transformation. Transformation requires guidance. Guidance demands leaders.

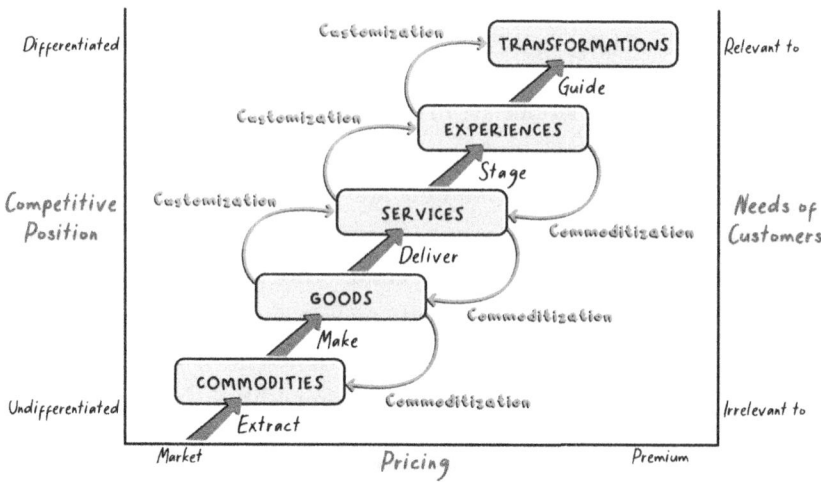

B. Pine II & J. Gilmore (2013). The Experience Economy: Past, Present and Future.

A progressive coach with a strong member culture is a wise investment: of your attention, your time, your money, your commitment. Be willing to pay money to be part of the right group, which saves you time and energy by pointing your attention and guiding you to what you want next, without the distractions and inevitable wrong-turns of trying to get there on your own. Invest in a guide so that you will show up—not just *think about* showing up.

You more easily find the guide and growth network for what you need next. Or, you stick around because you've found a *community of belonging* where you can be vulnerable and alive to your growing edge. Invest to be with people who make you uplevel your cognitive function, intuition, and feel-good longevity habits. Exploratory body wisdom is a wise investment. Be willing to throw down for that.

In traditional systems of medicine (TSMs) there's also awareness and mapping of the subtle body, spiritual evolution, and learning from masters. This becomes the next horizon of guided transformation that integrates ethos into subtle realms and higher orders of interconnectivity. There are layers within the landscape, higher orders of magnitude to verify. Enlightenment to be experienced.

By investing in yourself, you improve at investing in yourself. You get sharper at calculating the return on investing in who you want to become next. You stop delaying or hesitating as you get results from being in the right group, with the right guide, who helps you step into your better future faster.

A guide leads you back to yourself and helps you expand your experiences into domains that are hard to find—let alone navigate— without guidance. The more effective (and more fun) path to wisdom is with a good guide; a visionary who has activated a dynamic group to uplevel wisdom more effectively.

Value Your Future

Once you value yourself, you can assess yourself and your future as your best asset. Your life depends on how you invest your time, energy, attention, as well as money. Figure out what your health and life goals are worth to you. You have a body, a mind, and a soul with a purpose that needs valuation and investment to generate the future you want, aka a return on investment (ROI).

- Within a timeline, give yourself a budget to invest in your specific body and life goals.
- Review the chapter on PURPOSE and FOCUS.
- Find an expert coach or training program that is a good fit for your next goals.
- Find a coaching group that chases fulfillment and has the habits you want to develop. You'll get to habit automation around what matters most, faster.

Let's next consider who loses money when you rewild your habits; who profits when your money loses value due to inflation; and who makes money from chronic inflammation.

In the next chapter, I'll show you where you'll find the money.

---

1. Peter Block. "Community: The Structure of Belonging." Abundant Community. 16 July 2018, www.abundantcommunity.com/community-the-structure-of-belonging/. Accessed 24 Apr. 2022.
2. Block. "Community", 20.

Money

For health you must pay out of pocket.

In this chapter you'll investigate how you use money. We'll also look at the macro-trends of how we as a species invest, spend, and vote with our dollars—and from that perspective, who is winning, who is losing, and why that matters.

What represents money—i.e. exchange value—changes as humans evolve; each change makes it easier and faster for us to exchange more often, with less ritual. At the core, money is a *ritual of exchange*. If you couldn't exchange money, it wouldn't be worth anything. Money is how we count value, store value, trade value.

Your money represents what you value. What you value evolves as your habits evolve. In our coaching groups around the globe, we notice how primal habits drive down short-term consumerism and negative stressor purchases; and drive up smart long-term investments. When I polled my community for citizen data on the effects of becoming *uninflamed*, here is what they reported:

Reduced Consumption

- Eat less. Buy less food. No food waste.
- Buy fewer drugs and synthetic pharmaceutical products.
- Less interested in reading studies on sick-care or disease.
- Buy fewer skin products and body products.
- Buy less alcohol.
- Buy less "stuff" in general.
- Stopped buying conventional (non-organic) food grown with glyphosate (roundup), including processed foods, or foods containing preservatives.
- Buy less fast food, junk food, factory-farmed food, food with sugar, poor-quality vegetable oils.
- Buy fewer packaged drinks with chemicals or sweeteners.
- Buy fewer chemical household cleaning products.
- Pay less attention to alarmist news and media outlets, invest less time listening to conventional advertising.
- Invest less in conventional investment portfolios.
- Buy less conventional education degrees.
- Minimalist mindset: stuff takes time and attention away from focus and purpose.

Smarter Investments

- Buy higher quality stuff—from natural fiber clothing to home goods.
- Buy better food—more whole foods closer to source, with fewer middlemen and processing.
- Cook for themselves or hire personal chefs/prep chefs.
- Buy more plant foods, plant supplements, plant medicines, superfoods, probiotics, and fermented foods. Start growing and preserving homemade food by gardening, composting, sprouting, fermenting, and food-drying.
- Invest more directly in people, communities, ecosystems, local farms.
- Start buying organic, enzyme or plant-based cleaning products.
- Invest in personal body wisdom and health coaching (wellcare vs healthcare).
- Invest in wellness services, not beauty services.
- Invest in education and specific training for personal and professional goals.

- Invest in advisors, consultants, and coaches for career, finance, relationships, and life goals.
- Interested in serving their community by investing their time.
- Invest attention in one human species, one-planet solutions-based research, media, and companies.

People with primal habits invest smarter.

Primal habits evolve the consumer: they become the creator, the collaborator, the connector, the bestower of gifts. People invest time, money, and attention living their goals.

As money theorist Robert Breedlove points out: we end up making more of whatever we monetize.

WHO IS WINNING?

We monetize disease. In this section, we'll look at the "winners" in the chronic disease economy. It'll be no surprise that we'll talk about big pharma, advertising, and subsidized commodities.

Disease-care is winning.

Under the guise of "healthcare" we incentivize companies to make drugs for chronic diseases. We prioritize taxpayer dollars for sick-care rather than healing in our healthcare systems.[1] We also monetize our research institutes to concern themselves with researching diseases and drugs. Our taxpayer dollars don't go to our national institutes for research on healing and health. Nor are many of the studies funded by taxpayer dollars available to taxpayers. We make more "sick" with sick-care, more disease with disease-care. Citizens use "healthcare" for "sick visits," or acute inflammations of chronic conditions. Let's not kid ourselves, it's not health care.

In the U.S. alone, chronic inflammation diseases account for nearly 86% of aggregate healthcare spending.[2] People who are chronically inflamed use over 75% of all hospital days, office visits, home healthcare, and prescription drugs. One policy institute took a stab at estimating the cost of chronic issues on GDP. In 2020, they landed at $3.7 trillion each year, approximately 1/5 of the USA's GDP. Since 2010, 99% of Medicare and over 80% of Medicaid have gone towards sick-care for chronic.

Advertising is winning.

Modern culture has expectations that are shaped by the dramatic civilization-saving results that antibiotics and vaccines brought to acute infections. Yet, almost half of all advertising dollars on prescription drugs are to sell dramatic "solutions" to chronic conditions like arthritis, diabetes, and depression.[3] If these drugs worked to reverse the underlying chronic inflammation, that would be swell. However, they don't uproot the tidal wave of underlying diet and lifestyle habits that generate chronic inflammation. The research shows pharmaceuticals are over-prescribed as an immediate, simplistic solution. They are prescribed for more conditions than the research shows they are effective for, claims are exaggerated and they can be unsafe.[4]

If you've been exposed to mainstream advertising lately, you're well aware of the "gloom to bloom" ads, the psych-ops to persuade people to ask their doctor for drugs. Direct-to-consumer advertising for pharmaceuticals and surgical procedures influences citizens to act as consumers of magic-bullet medicine, not preventative medicine or real healing.

It turns out that patent medicine manufacturers pioneered modern advertising over 100 years ago in America. Advertising makes money from pharma and vice versa, while the citizen loses.[5] The trend is global. We are susceptible to buying more drugs to reverse the damage of previous drugs—as seen in the innovative and exciting microbiome-regenerating drugs (see MICROBIOME, EAT DIRTY). Yet, this is an example of a drug that might actually repair the underlying microbiome depletion of chronic inflammation.

Vaccines are winning.

Vaccines have undoubtedly been lifesavers for humanity. But vaccines should be accompanied by public service messages and support on how to proactively reduce chronic inflammation at the same time, because they are far more effective when the body is unburdened by inflammation. Citizens should also be given the freedom to choose, rather than having vaccination enforced by mandate. That would be helpful.

In 2021, a record 493 new billionaires were minted, propelled by unprecedented money printing under the guise of "economic stimulus" in response to the COVID epidemic. Among those newcomers are at least 40 new entrants who draw their fortunes from companies involved in monetizing Covid-19. The money wasn't made from generating products and services to reduce the inflammation problem for people who suffered the most: those with co-morbidities.[6]

Subsidized crops are winning.

What happens when governments interfere with their food supply via subsidies? What happens when we don't place financial value on "the commons," the shared natural resources, like clean rivers, clean air, clean oceans, and healthy, microbe-rich soil?

A subsidy is essentially a cash payment to a specific industry to lower the price of a commodity; it's paid for by citizens (via taxes) and controlled by government policy. Subsidies come directly as a cash infusion or tax break, or indirectly through marketing assistance loans, domestic production limits, and import quotas.

For example, the US and Europe subsidize the "Big Five": corn, soybeans, wheat, cotton, and rice. If indirect subsidies were taken into account, sugar would make the top five, at least in the US. Corn and soy are primarily fed to cattle, and so are subsidized, non-organic, conventional feedlot livestock farming.

Of course, the most heavily subsidized crops are those that are most often turned into ultra-processed foods. An ultra-processed food bears very little resemblance to its original crop and is highly dosed with sugar, salt, fat, and preservatives. Some "food" is so processed that it is turned into an indigestible toxin that no human should go near—high fructose corn syrup and hydrogenated corn oil are examples. Ultra-processed food leads to food addiction, which leads to insulin resistance.

Ultra-processed foods are notoriously low in fiber. You stretch your stomach to feel the pleasure of fullness, which used to come from fiber-rich foods (fibre adds bulk). You keep buying more, and stretching more, which develops leptin resistance, so you can't tell when you're full. These are biological indicators of malfunction. When you stretch beyond the breaking point you generate transactions in the disease-care system. Today, close to 60% of the average American's diet is ultra-processed, which means ultra-subsidized—and unfortunately for us, this means ultra-inflammation.

Each country seems to have their weakness. The Philippines is the #1 rice subsidizer, and 30% of Filipino adolescents will be overweight and obese by 2030.[7]

Notice how consumption of ultra-processed ingredients follows a very similar curve to that of chronic disease.

Prior to the modern situation, sugar was subsidized by slave labor. Before that, sugar wasn't a commodity. Vegetable oil was invented as a potential commodity in a German lab in 1907. Oils are hydrogenated to prolong shelf life, which renders them indigestible trans fats. When you cover it up with sugar and salt, it's harder for you to taste that you are not eating food. Europe is trying to make trans fats illegal to produce. Thanks for leading the way. Notably, specialized crops—including fruits, vegetables, and nutrient-diverse superfoods which act like supplements—receive very little subsidies, so prices push real nutrition out of reach.

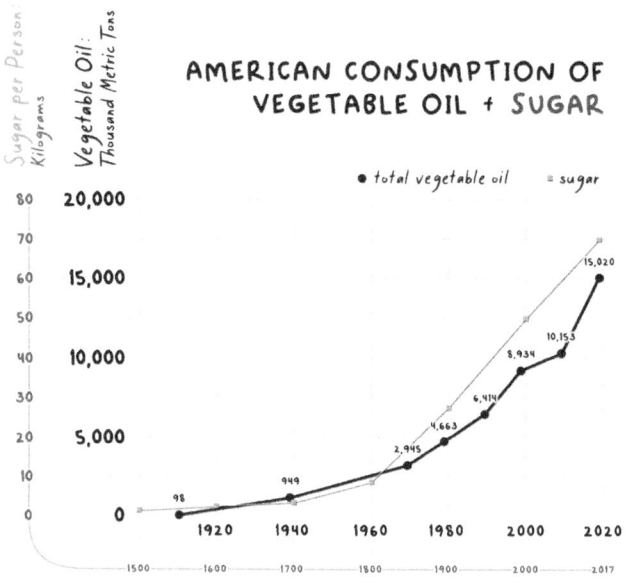

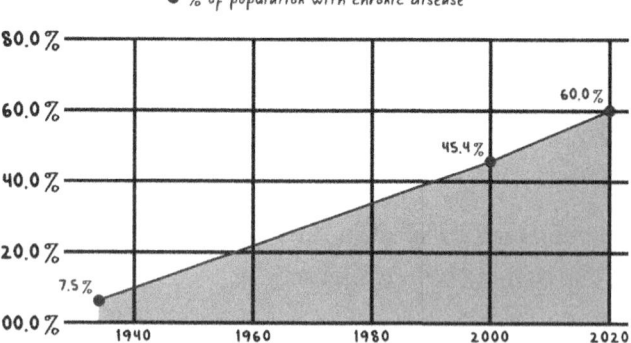

Lobbying groups, special interests, and profiting parties are the middlemen that ensure the subsidies stick. Middlemen cost money. Subsidies and the hidden costs of bureaucracy confuse value in the digital age. Across the planet, these are the most abundant crops we grow, which in turn generate demand for toxic chemical fertilizers and pesticides. Feed subsidies for conventional, large feedlot beef farming also privilege this method over pasture feeding. Which, in turn, generates chemical runoff into what is ultimately the drinking water for all ecosystems.

As citizens, we invest in sickness with our attention and our tax dollars. United, we spend on chronic inflammation. Together, we feel like crap.

NO ONE IS REALLY WINNING—WE'RE FRAGILE.

This is from an interview between economist Eric Weinstein and AI expert, Lex Fridman:

WEINSTEIN: *It does not appear that we found a way to grow anything organic, and good, and decent that we need right now. And that's kind of the key issue.*

FRIDMAN: *So who is the we?*

WEINSTEIN: *Those of us who wish to have a future for our great-grandchildren. Let's take the subset of people who are worried about things long after their demise.*[8]

Past generations to future generations connect through you, right now.

Evolutionary human communities are ethical organizations that value the long-term investment horizon. Today, the global economic system incentivizes rapacious corporate boards to seize planetary resources and human freedoms by driving inflationary spending and growing governments. Later in the interview with Fridman, Weinstein states:

I don't think that economists understand what a price index is that measures inflation. Nor do I think that economists understand what a growth index or a quantity index is that measures GDP... They are intellectually not in a position to manage their own field.

We take turns printing money for conventional banking, big pharma, defense, agriculture, and health care. If you can't evolve the system, evolve yourself and your community (see WISDOM, LEAD).

WHO IS LOSING?

We all see the bloat, the distress, the dis-ease people carry today. While we often subscribe to the idea of "progress," and are led to believe that our nations and societies keep forging ever on, ever up, toward greater wealth, technological utopia, and longer, better lives, our eating habits tell a different story.

Babies are now born with chronic inflammation and poor neuroplasticity.[9] We're robbing ourselves of our own hard-won genetic intelligence. Who else is losing?

- Small-scale organic farmers
- Fruit and vegetable crops
- Ecosystems around the planet
- Holistic medicine practitioners who aren't covered by sick-care insurance policies
- Your children or grandchildren
- You
- Me

As a species, we are bankrupting ourselves. As citizen-taxpayers, we all subsidize and suffer from the chronic inflammation economy. There is no ROI for the citizens. People suffer daily, babies born tomorrow never get a shot at true well-being, and a few people get very rich with money that won't transfer value to their great-grandchildren on a fragile planet. Conventional habits eclipse joie de vivre, turning life into a trainwreck. As Alan Watts said, "The paper in our system becomes more valuable than the wealth."[10]

So, what do *you* value?

Invest in your values with your habits, your actions, your attention, your votes, your money, to spread true value.

YOU AS WINNER = YOU AS LEADER

So, how do *you* win?

Cultivate your primal habits, and community will appear around you. Habits are not just cultural—habits are communal. Just as your microbiome is your unique culture, your macrobiome is the community around you. Your habits reveal your rhythm, your level of consciousness or mindset, your microbiome, your connection, your vibe, your health, your community. Primal-ness cultivates a culture within and around you.

Primal habits reverse the trend that turns citizens into consumers and potential leaders into victims. Non-essentials that get in the way of authentic voice and natural power disappear from life. Clear the clutter. Regenerate the intelligent design of your physiology and psychology. Run your high-tech human biochemistry like a professional.

As you live the primal habits, they rub off on those around you.

Notice who shows up.

The more primal your habits, the more you realize you are leading, and you must lead. Your regenerative habits become a pull for your core people to reverse the tide of chronic inflammation. The people in your circles have a lifesaver in you. You restore humanity to the humans in your life. Lead your people. Your vision of a better life for yourself, a better community for your kids or grandkids, a better world... making that real is your next potential. Become the leader we need you to be.

Own your reality to create the next better one. Become a leader with purpose, with focus, in every situation in your life.

So, root your rhythm. Align actions to vision. Gain abilities you don't have. Turn up your cognitive function. Think smarter. Feel better. Bump your consciousness up to the next dimension of higher order.

Join us.

1. Robert Breedlove. "Strategy, Capital, and Bitcoin with Mike Alfred (WiM113)." YouTube. 19 Jan. 2022, www.youtube.com/watch?v=TOdLFvP-TQ4. Accessed 24 Apr. 2022.

2. Halsted R. Holman. "The Relation of the Chronic Disease Epidemic to the Health Care Crisis." ACR Open Rheumatology, vol. 2, no. 3, 2020, pp. 167–73. doi:10.1002/acr2.11114.

3. L. Torres. "Medicare Spent Bulk of Drug Cash on Advertised Products." Bloomberg Law. 1 Jan. 2021, news.bloomberglaw.com/health-law-and-business/medicare-spent-bulk-of-drug-spending-on-advertised-products. Accessed 20 Apr. 2022.

4. F. Fani Marvasti, Stafford RS. From sick care to health care-reengineering prevention into the U.S. system. N Engl J Med. 2012 Sep 6;367(10):889-91. doi: 10.1056/NEJMp1206230. PMID: 22931257; PMCID: PMC4339086; Clarke, Janice L et al. "An Innovative Approach to Health Care Delivery for Patients with Chronic Conditions." Population health management vol. 20,1 (2017): 23-30. doi:10.1089/pop.2016.0076.

5. "Cures and Curses: A History of Pharmaceutical Advertising in America." University of St. Augustine for Health Sciences Library. 1 Jan. 2022, library.usa.edu/Cures-Curses-Exhibit. Accessed 23 Apr. 2022.

6. Giacomo Tognini. "Meet the 40 New Billionaires Who Got Rich Fighting Covid-19." Forbes. 6 Apr. 2021, www.forbes.com/sites/giacomotogni-ni/2021/04/06/meet-the-40-new-billionaires-who-got-rich-fighting-covid-19/?sh=79a4841b17e5. Accessed 20 Apr. 2022; Lex Fridman. "Eric Weinstein: Difficult Conversations, Freedom of Speech, and Physics | Lex Fridman Podcast #163." YouTube. 23 Feb. 2021, www.youtube.com/watch?v=ifX_JnBfxTY&ab_chan-nel=LexFridman. Accessed 24 Apr. 2022.

7. "Everybody Needs to Act to Curb Obesity: DOH and Development Partners Call for a Whole-of-society Approach to Reduce Obesity in the Philippines." *Unicef*, 4 Mar. 2022, www.unicef.org/philippines/press-releases/everybody-needs-act-curb-obesity.

8. Lex Fridman. "Eric Weinstein: Difficult Conversations, Freedom of Speech, and Physics | Lex Fridman Podcast #163." YouTube. 23 Feb. 2021,

www.youtube.com/watch?v=ifX_JnBfxTY&ab_channel=LexFridman. Accessed 24 Apr. 2022.

9. M. I. Goran, et al. "Effects of Consuming Sugars and Alternative Sweeteners During Pregnancy on Maternal and Child Health: Evidence for a Secondhand Sugar Effect." The Proceedings of the Nutrition Society, vol. 78, no. 3, 2019, pp. 262–71. doi:10.1017/S002966511800263X.

10. Your Universe. "Alan Watts ∞ Look Beyond Your Mental Condition." YouTube. 30 Nov. 2018, www.youtube.com/watch?v=N9hgCAR5VdU. Accessed 20 Apr. 2022.

CATE

CATE STILLMAN devoted her life to planetary thrive as a teenager. Her path brought her through working in global warming policy to a deep dive into how to evolve human consciousness.

She hosts the Thrive with Cate Podcast and Wellness Pro Academy podcast, weekly podcasts on thought leadership with simple solutions for humans to be healthier. Cate is the author of Uninflamed: 21 Primal Habits, Body Thrive and Master of You with Sounds True Publishing. An avid mountain biker, skier, and surfer, her family splits their time between Wyoming and Mexico. For free workshops, check out yogahealer.com and listen to her podcast.

ABOUT CLUB THRIVE:

CLUB THRIVE is for people who want to thrive in their bodies and lives.
CLUB HERO is for ambitious, innovative people curious to crush their unique life goals, purpose, or mission and become masters of identity evolution.

Want to connect? Please email us: curious@clubthrive.global

ABOUT WELLNESS PRO ACADEMY

WELLNESS PRO ACADEMY is a training program that guides wellness professionals into a better business model, better client results, and a great work/life balance lifestyle. The academy guides you to:

- Guide your club based on your wellness wisdom
- Guide your members into the circadian rhythm habits
- Launch your pilot CLUB through the stages of Attract, Engage, Enroll, Onboard
- Refine your process to lead members to wellness faster
- Refine your marketing and sales process to sell out seats

Every member is trained in the CLUB business model in real time. The academy is built for new members to earn a return on investment in the first few months up to the first year. Some members quadruple their tuition investment in the first quarter year. All members love the transition from teaching into leading the transformational journey.

Get into LEAD YOUR CLUB for free here: —> www.wellnesspro.
academy/leader
PROMO code: PRO497

Printed in Great Britain
by Amazon

36745896R00128